Minimalist Home Secrets

The Ultimate Guide to Declutter and Organize Your Home
Through Minimalist Living

By

Grace Burke

MINIMALIST HOME SECRETS
First edition. October 18, 2019.

Table of Contents

Introduction

I inherited my 3,000 square foot clutter-filled home from my mother when she passed away. When some children inherit their parents' homes with their contents, they call in a service to catalogue and tag items to sell. They talk to a real estate agent about listing the house. They talk through division of profits with other heirs. Unfortunately, there was none of that when I found out the house was mine. My mother's house was thoughtfully built as a retreat for immediate family and to accommodate family members during important holidays. It wasn't supposed to be near a major metropolitan area and it wasn't meant to be sold off to provide a nest egg to anyone in my family. The house contained the clutter of countless possessions of my mother and past generations. It contained pieces I remember growing up with and ones more recently salvaged and made new again. It wasn't going to be a cut and dry inheritance. It was going to be so much more.

Soon after receiving the keys, I found myself standing in the entrance feeling both emotional and overwhelmed. Each item was brought here by my mother's hand, but altogether, the clutter was too much. Too much to allow myself and the rest of the family peace when staying here. Too much to wrangle in a weekend of furiously packing boxes. This house needed more than the conventional walk-through and gathering of favorite pieces before selling off the rest. It needed a heavy dose of minimalism.

It was fairly easy deciding to keep the house rather than sell it. It maintains its own charm sitting nestled in the mountains with trees lined around it. Winter nights deliver such a remarkable stillness you feel as though you're the only being left on Earth. When the wind whips through the lush trees on a summer afternoon, you feel revitalized. The decision to keep the house was easy, but accepting the task of applying minimalist principles was a bit daunting. There were many items in the home I knew could never leave. There were other items, however, that still held important meaning in the family, but did not serve a purpose anymore. Unfortunately, that distinction was lost when I found everything piled together and covered in a layer of dust. In its current state, there was no way to honor the special pieces and separate them from curbside finds. Accepting that fact, I found applying minimalist principles to my mother's house was the best way to bestow honor on family heirlooms. It would allow me to bring focus to the pieces that represented us best and to the items that serve us well.

Honoring my family's pieces was important, but I wasn't looking to build a museum. I wanted the house to fulfill its original purpose as a gathering place for family. I wanted to see twenty or so family members seated around the dining table originally used to feed workers on my great-grandmother's farm. I desired each of the bedrooms perfectly appointed for peaceful rest. I envisioned the grand living room hosting family for game night while a fire in the hearth kept us warm. The goal I envisioned would bring the serenity and respite one expects from a vacation home. The practice of minimalism helped me achieve my goal and this book is here to help you achieve your own.

I found my family especially supportive of my goal. They, too, could see how the clutter and extraneous items distracted from the beauty of the home. The prospect of retreating to the home on holidays and finding comfortable uncluttered surroundings was irresistible to them. It was time to get started. Items not suitable for hosting family were donated to charity or sold. Some items called out to be given to family and friends as reminders of their relationship with my mother. For all the physical and financial gain, this particular emotional gain stands out as a highlight. I even found new homes for items I had moved in with, but ended up being duplicates. When finding homes for these duplicates, I considered their usefulness for the intended recipient. I had found a new balance in my relationship with objects in my home and wanted to make sure I didn't tip the balance of someone else's home with my gift.

I knew my experience practicing minimalism in my new-to-me home contained many lessons others would find helpful. I wrote this book with those lessons in mind. Each chapter can help you methodically transform your home into a place of peace, gratification, and purposeful living. For our purposes, "Minimalism" simply means movement toward simplicity and away from consumerism. The push and pull actions inside the definition lead to balance. Balance that can fuel a more fulfilled life. Even if you aren't a devotee to modern minimalism, this book contains lessons to benefit all homeowners.

You may have tried a minimalist approach before and found it too daunting. Or perhaps you're like me and received an inheritance of clutter. It may be your first foray into the practice of minimalism. Wherever you begin, the words on these pages will support you in letting go of unnecessary items. You'll learn how to part with the many extraneous heirlooms passed down from generations before you. You will learn the best strategies to avoid overspending and discover actionable steps to open up every room in your home.

Minimalism is not synonymous with perfection. Modern minimalist living is a practice of awareness and intention regarding your belongings, time, and energy. By practicing minimalism, it becomes the lens through which we see the world and ourselves. It creates alignment with the objects in our lives and our purpose. When I stand in my mother's house now, I see only the best representations of her and our family. Before, my relationship with the objects in the house and the purpose I envisioned was out of alignment. Frustration and stress levels both ran high.

As I moved further along in my practice, I found physical benefits in addition to emotional and financial ones. I'm amazed at how quickly I can clean my house now that extraneous furniture and clutter has moved on. I never worry about unexpected guests or last-minute dinners with friends because my house stays cleaner for longer. The compliments I receive on the new layout of furniture and the exhibition of prized family heirlooms motivates me to continue this practice. The physical calmness I gain from more clear space on the walls and floors is immeasurable.

The changes in my emotional well-being as a result of decluttering are not unique. A 2009 UCLA study "No Place Like Home" linked the association of words like "clutter" and "unfinished" with one's home as indicative of that person's stress level. The frequency of word usage was shown to have a direct effect on the release of the stress hormone cortisol. The way we see our home and our objects really does correlate with our mood, and thus our emotional well-being.

A different study conducted by psychologist and researcher NiCole R. Keith, Ph.D. at Indiana University found that tidier homes increased an individiual's level of physical activity, thereby reducing the risk for cardiovascular disease. This conclusion took the study by surprise as it looked at the many factors that impact a person's level of physical activity. A positive attitude about the space we inhabit can affect our physical health just as it affects our emotional health.

You chose this book because you're tired of tripping over clutter at every turn. You're finished with overpacked closets that provide nothing in the way of organization or functionality. You've taken multitudes of items to local charities only to see more items creep in to your home. You're ready to walk into your home and feel peace, not a sense of dread from mountains of clutter. You're searching for the contentment of a well-organized home. This book is here to guide you on your journey to the serenity you seek.

There's never been a better time to get started as the waves of consumerism grow larger than ever. We're constantly receiving advertisements to purchase more items, to solve our problems with one more piece of clutter. It's time to turn away from the weight of the consumerist life and move towards a sense of harmony that comes from minimalism. This book contains everything you need to find balance in your relationship with the pieces in your home.

I'm excited for you to begin this journey and experience revitalization, one room at a time.

Chapter 1. Letting Go
Essential Mental Shifts You Need

Each chapter in this book contains vital information to help you practice modern minimalism successfully. In this first chapter, the most important power mindsets are laid out for you to absorb and manifest at the very start of your journey. In order to adjust the objects in your home, you must first adjust your mindset toward them. Different objects require different lines of thinking and in this chapter you'll find successful strategies to part with anything. I had many family heirlooms in my home, but I also had items like a faded favorite dress that still held a place in my heart. Knowing how to interact with each object made my 3,000 square foot project bearable. It will help make yours bearable, as well.

Power Mindset 1 - "Always be Thankful"

Gratitude is one of the strongest emotions and one of the most transformative. We experience gratitude as an instant emotion upon receiving a gift or other positive gesture. We can also practice it, which is encouraged for those seeking more balance in their life. Practicing gratitude with the objects in our homes helps bring balance between the objects and your purpose. It is the first power mindset because it underlies the entire practice of modern minimalism. Gratitude for our homes and their contents is what allows us to move forward in the practice.

To practice this mindset, take a step outside of the room you're about to begin organizing. Before entering, deeply inhale and exhale for 10 breaths. I want you to calm your heart as well as your thoughts. Step through the entrance to the room and stand in the middle. Look at all of the objects and furniture as you slowly turn about the room. Think of the many ways in which these items found their way into your home. The friends and family who gifted you with an item. The promotion at work that led you to purchase an item as celebration. The worn out items that have given you all their use. Be thankful for their contributions to your space and your life.

Once you have done that, begin with one item at a time. Hold it, remember its origin, and be thankful for its service to you. Even if you don't intend to get rid of an item, you want to renew your gratitude for it. By giving it recognition, you're bestowing positivity that will collect with the positivity from other items in your home. This helps support the peace and calm you seek from organizing your home.

We come by the objects in our homes in various ways: inheritance, gifts, our own selection and purchase. The power mindset, "Always Be Thankful," can be used for any object, but is especially powerful when applied to objects given to us. We often find it difficult to get rid of something that was a gift. Especially if we see the giver on a regular basis. But it is not possible to keep every gift ever given to us. Even though items are no longer in your physical possession, you remain grateful for having received them. The emotion of gratitude lasts far beyond the physical object.

Power Mindset 2 - "I'll Get Something Better"

How many times have you rifled through your medicine cabinet or clothes dresser and found items that you bought because they were needed at the time? Maybe it's a $1 comb picked up in a Chicago drugstore when the wind got the best of your hair right before a big meeting. Or maybe it's a cheap tourist sweatshirt purchased out of frigid desperation on a trip to the nation's capital. Whatever the circumstances, whatever the object, there's a time, and a power mindset, to help you let go. "I'll Get Something Better" is best applied to objects that you haven't used for at least 90 days.

You'll find yourself using this mindset as you dig deeper into closets and explore rooms you haven't entered in days. You find items that you cherished enough to store safely, along with, the same reasons to keep it again. With each item you find during your practice, assess the last time you used it and the potential for using it in the next 90 days. If you haven't used something for 90 days, its purpose to you has dissipated into clutter. Be thankful for what it has done for you and open your space by removing it from your home. If you do need it again in the future, you'll be able to replace it with something better than what you had.

Power Mindset 3 - "Clinging To An Item Lowers Its Value"

In college, I impulsively bought a dress from one of the big fast-fashion brands during a shopping trip with one of my best friends. The first time I wore it, I received a multitude of attention and compliments. I relished the confidence I felt, especially as an awkward college freshman trying to find my way. It's been years since college, and even more time has passed since the shopping trip that delivered such a dress. Yet, it remained in my closet. When integrating my possessions into my new home, I felt the weight of dragging the dress with me wherever I went. All of the warm fuzzy feelings I used to feel when holding the fabric in my hands were replaced by feelings of weariness. I was weary at having carried it with me for so long and weary from the crushing reality of the project I was taking on with my new home. The value this dress held for decades deflated faster than a bunch of balloons in a nail factory.

By clinging to this dress, I diminished its own value. The truth is, if you hold onto everything because it is special, then nothing is ever *uniquely* special.

Practicing this power mindset may seem daunting. There are countless birthday cards, letters, gifts, memorabilia, and more tugging at you. It's important to remember, however, why you began this journey. You might be looking for a new start. Or you felt that clutter was beginning to control your life. Whatever the reason for starting, we're all looking for the same effect: peace, clarity, and serenity. These are the direct results of practicing minimalism. Keep them in mind as you practice and pair it with each power mindset, to reach the goal you've set for yourself.

90/90 Rule

These power mindsets lay the foundation for your approach to clutter in your home. As you get into your practice, there's one more tool you should keep close: the 90/90 rule.

Joshua Fields Millburn and Ryan Nicodemus share this rule on their blog, The Minimalists, and iterations of it can be found elsewhere. When holding an item, ask yourself the last time you used it. If it has been more than 90 days and you don't see yourself using it in the next 90 days, then it goes. Letting it go means that the space it occupied is now clear and if you do find you need it in the future, you can get a better one.

This rule also acts as a thread of motivation throughout the practice of minimalism. Even if you are approaching your home in small increments, you are still prone to being overwhelmed. By having this rule at the ready, you can quickly decide if a random object is worth keeping or not. The prospect of getting a new one in the future, should you need it, also makes the rule easy to apply. So many consumer products and tools get better over time. Chances are you could find a higher quality replacement at a lower cost, should you ever need an item again.

Family Heirlooms

We've gone through the junk drawers, closets, under-bed storage, and can even see a clean garage on the horizon. But in all of those places, family heirlooms lurk demanding attention. These objects can be some of the most emotional to part with and let go. We often feel a sense of responsibility for these objects and that the burden is on us to preserve them for the next generation. To help you sort through family heirlooms, I've created several categories of items and how to approach organizing them or giving them away.

China, Flatware, and Other Dining Ware

If you are the recipient of a china set, flatware, or various kitchen utensils and tools, congratulations! These may be some of the more useful family heirlooms to receive. However, staring into the pattern of a dessert plate with the intentions of throwing more gatherings is not the same as regularly hosting more events. Sort through each piece and see how it might replace an item you currently own or how it would add to your routine. Consider also where it would live when not in use. Assuming you won't be using bone china with gilded edges as everyday plates, you want to store what you keep in an accessible location. You also want to make sure it doesn't crowd the items used on a daily basis.

Clothing, Jewelry and Accessories

Vintage clothing, jewelry, and accessories are constantly coming back into style. You may have several pieces, pillbox hats, 50's baubles, or a Pendleton suit that were once part of a family member's wardrobe. Clothing like this may especially be difficult to part with because you might have memories of the person wearing it and they're no longer here. Unless these items can fit into your current wardrobe and style, it doesn't make sense to store them indefinitely. There are many people who wear vintage clothes exclusively and would love the chance to own these items. Feel confident knowing those people will take pride in wearing the items and take care of them. Local vintage stores or even a consignment store can take these items for you and do the heavy lifting of finding their new owners. If your supply is dense and you have the time, you may also want to open an online store on an existing platform to list and sell the items. Donating to the costume shop of a local theatre or school's art program would also find new life for these items.

Furniture (Both Small and Large)

Furniture styles range so drastically just in the last 100 years. Mid-century modern was sold at the same time another furniture maker was reviving Queen Anne style dining chairs. If you receive furniture, large or small, carefully consider their purpose and how they might be of help to you in your organized home. A secretary desk may replace one you currently own and provide proper storage for everything in your home office. A tall buffet that used to hold China may serve you better as a bookcase in a reading nook you set up for yourself.

If there are pieces that don't match your decor or won't be able to serve a purpose in your organized home, it's okay to let it go. Depending on the style and condition, there may be specific collectors who would love to own the pieces. You can contact a local antique dealer for help finding a buyer or if you would like to make a philanthropic gesture, donate the furniture. Organizations that build homes for low-income families can sell the furniture to support their mission or place them into the homes themselves.

Home Decor

This category can be expansive. Vase collections. Plant stands. Paperweights galore. Since there are so many elements of home décor, deciding which ones to keep can be daunting. If you've inherited these items you've received little pieces of the home your relatives made for themselves. This in no way means you need to assume their aesthetic as a way of honoring them. Find what fits into your style and what you can realistically house. Then, let the rest go.

Chapter 2. Minimalist Shopping
How To Transform Your Spending Habits

As I talked about in the introduction, this book is about finding the balance between the objects you own and your intent. An essential part of maintaining that balance is to transform your spending habits.

As I began the process of decluttering my home, a heavy thought hit me: What's to stop the house from filling up again with *more* things? The halls of consumerism surround me everyday. The grocery store now sells seasonal home décor. A simple trip to a big box store to check off my list of needs turns into a mental war against bringing home every other thing I see. I needed to do more than I'd ever done to ensure my practice of minimalism in this new home was not in vain. In this chapter, I put together the best ideas to avoid the pitfalls of consumerism and ensure success in your own practice.

The average American household spends $18,000 each year on nonessentials. This includes everything from subscription boxes of beauty goods to expensive dinners. We buy new outfits for a special occasion despite already owning several that would suit. We let ourselves wander through the bargain area at the front of our favorite big box store only to walk away with handfuls of goods. We upgrade items in our homes not because the old version is broken, but because it is no longer the newest model.

Our collective habit of consumerism opens the flood gates to clutter in our homes. You may often find yourself receiving a new Amazon box before you've even had a chance to recycle the one you received just last week. You upgrade your blow dryer because you found a good deal and decide to hold onto your old one "just in case." Before you know it, your drawers and cabinets are full. Your mind begins to lose the peace and serenity of an organized home. You lose track of recent purchases amongst all the chaos of clutter.

It's not difficult to see the correlation between bringing things into your home and increasing the overall clutter. There is a financial side effect, however, that is both shocking and even a little upsetting: 60% of adults lack the savings to cover a $1,000 expense. This is a direct result of Americans' yearly spend on nonessentials. The most worrisome part of this statistic is that a $1000 expense is not wholly uncommon. A car repair or unexpected medical bill could easily hover around that mark. A much-needed home repair or appliance breakdown could also wipe out limited savings. I have dealt with my own fair share of new car brakes and lawnmower breakdowns. It was impossible to handle those unexpected expenses without my savings.

I don't bring all of this up to scare you or discourage you from your practice. On the contrary, these numbers should encourage you on your journey. I want them to motivate you to continue what you started and affirm your decision to take the momentous step of opening yourself to modern minimalism. Our modern consumer-based culture is at odds with minimalist living, it's an enemy of the practice. The financial consequences impact not only your wallet, but your peace of mind. The peace and serenity sought from practicing minimalism is crushed under the weight of the consumer mindset pressed upon us. Acknowledging that and carrying it with you through your practice protects you like a piece of armor.

Shop and Buy With Intention

One of the lasting childhood memories I have of my late mother is shopping. Sometimes it would just be a trip to the grocery store to pick up our staples for lunch and dinner throughout the week. Occasionally it would be a quick trip to the mall for new gym shorts. A particularly exciting shopping adventure happened every year, right at the end of summer. We'd pack up in the family van and drive to the local outlet mall to cover our back-to-school shopping. We had our list of stores we'd visit each year and depending on what we found each time, we'd cut a few from the list for that year. I looked forward to the fresh start of a new wardrobe each year and it was justifiable to meet the needs of my growing body. As I got older, I still loved the tradition of a yearly trip to the mall for several new items to add to my closet. I was even envious of a cousin who went to New York City each summer for new clothes.

Before I began my practice of minimalist living, I let the behaviors from childhood seep into my adult lifestyle. My voracious love for new clothes extended into all aspects of my adult life. New jobs meant new office supplies. A new year at college meant a new backpack and all new school supplies. But as an adult, the purchases didn't produce the same warm fuzzy feelings they did as a kid. Beyond the purchases necessary for living, everything else felt like a one-time high that quickly faded. It left behind way too many things and a closing in feeling that comes from having too much stuff around you.

The fact is we have to shop. We need to shop for food to eat, clothes to wear, and sometimes begrudgingly, a new car when ours gives out. But, that doesn't mean you need to give up practicing minimalism. I turned my own shopping habits around in my pursuit of a minimalist home and put together the 8 rules I live by to keep my home clutter-free.

Rule 1: Unsubscribe and Unfollow Retailers

It used to be easy to avoid the trumpet calls of our favorite stores. Those emails we received en masse from giving out our email at the register or online checkout could just be deleted. We could unsubscribe from the list and call it a day. Now, we need to do that and more. Every brand leverages the channels of social media to promote their products as well as that 4-letter angel's call: SALE. Instagram, Facebook, and even Twitter are flooded with aesthetically captivating content from brands.

They want you to reach into your wallet and immediately put in your credit card number for the latest fad or gadget.

The easiest way to remove the temptation is to unfollow brands and stores on all social media platforms. Yes, the sponsored ads they pay for will continue to pop up here and there. But, with constant updates on their feed, you're missing so much content that could tempt you into buying something you don't need.

Another option to take this rule a step further is train social media platforms on the ads you don't want to see. On Instagram, when you spot a Sponsored post, you can tap the three dots in the upper right corner of the post and select "Hide Ad." Instagram will provide you with a few feedback options and you can select "It's Not Relevant." This method will not get rid of every single Instagram ad, but it will help cut down on the brands that are your pressure points. The brands that you know grab you with their semi-annual sales or the ingenuity of their product line.

On Facebook, you can repeat this method in much the same way. Find a sponsored post, select the three dots in the upper righthand corner of the ad, and a drop down menu will appear. "Hide Ad" is the first selection and when you tap it, the ad will immediately disappear and Facebook records the request. A small pop-up will appear and you can select your reason for hiding the ad.

Rule 2: Stay Away From Cute Shopping Areas

They're an epidemic. Main Street Downtown in Anywhere, USA is full of endless enticing window displays. Handmade signs call out at you to "shop local!" and check out the newest wares. They almost beg you to let go of shopping guilt because everything is locally made, fairly traded, and did they mention organic? I live between two amazing downtown areas with everything I could ever want. But, I stay away on almost every occasion and have a strategy to minimize my time walking the historic brick sidewalks.

My strategy involves parking and utilizing it to keep me from spending extra time downtown. I often need to visit a government office or drop off library books, but there's no reason for me to spend additional time exploring the shops. I typically choose a parking spot (or pay for one!) that is the minimum time I need to complete my business downtown. Knowing there is a literal clock running, I complete my errands and return to my car. There's no time to see what's new at the kitchen store when I see parking enforcement making their usual rounds.

When I visit friends and family in larger cities, cars are a hassle. I like to take public transit to most every destination within a city. To help me avoid the same temptation in larger cities, I will keep an eye on the timetable for the bus or metro and try to complete any errands or necessary purchases in time to catch the next bus or train. I can adjust it based on my needs for each situation and it keeps me accountable.

Rule 3: Research What You Want to Buy

Part of buying with intention is knowing what you plan to purchase. It's imperative that in the buying process you learn as much as you can about the product you need to own. This will allow you to assess a potential purchase's added value to your home. Each item you bring into your home now should serve you well in its life.

Before I begin my online research or even asking friends who have purchased a similar item, I think about the pros and cons for purchasing it. I often find after completing this list I lack the real concrete use this item will fulfill. It's saved me from many purchases that would have served me poorly.

Internet marketing can sometimes add to the temptation of impulse buying. Advertisers on the web use cookies to track our movements. When we visit an Amazon page to look at reviews or go straight to the website of the brand of item we wish to purchase, they know. They use that knowledge to put banner ads on web pages we visit long after we've viewed their item. It's important to know this marketing tactic in order to stay accountable even when those pesky banner ads appear. Depending on your browser, you can even conduct your research using "incognito mode." This would allow you to search without the cookies being able to track your clicks when you return to the regular browser view.

Rule 4: Wait 48 Hours To Purchase

Good things come to those who wait. I'm a firm believer in this statement and find it best applies to minimalist shopping. I like to save the impulsive behavior for budgeting a vacation and choosing a destination at the last minute.

Waiting to make a purchase after you've decided on an item prevents you from regretting a purchase later. By not waiting and allowing the potential for regret, you may find yourself spending even more time by having to return it if it doesn't work out. Allowing yourself the space to think about your decision means you can weigh the purchase with a level head. It's easy to feel pressure to purchase something when a good deal comes up or when you find the perfect solution to an organizational problem in your home. Taking the time to let the decision rest will give you peace of mind and confidence when you do go to purchase the item.

Rule 5: Assess Your Buying Intentions

This rule takes the previous one a step further. Practicing modern minimalism requires a lot of intention. You're being intentional when it comes to what remains in your home and you should do the same with what enters. Whenever I want to purchase something new to bring into my home, I sit down and ask myself a few important questions.

Do I want this item because it will help me in my everyday life? How did I first decide I wanted this item? Did I hear an ad, see a sale, or hear about it from a friend? Do I own anything like it already that would serve the purpose I need?

The purpose of these questions isn't to interrogate yourself with every potential purchase. Instead, they're meant to get down to the core of your desire for the item. Practicing modern minimalism means we live with our best intentions, both for our home and for the items we bring into it. We all know the questions to ask ourselves to get to the root of why we desire what we do. Pulling those out while you're in the midst of shopping will ensure your potential purchase adds value to your life.

Rule 6: Make A List and Stick With It

I use this rule on a weekly basis. I make a list for my groceries and lists for trips to the bulk items store. The purpose of making a list is to help you stay accountable when you're standing in front of the attractive product displays or enticing checkout shelves.

My grocery list is ongoing, but when I plan a trip to the hardware store or a specialty store, it's usually for a specific project. I can often put together my rough list of items needed to complete a task thanks to research done beforehand. However, I prepare for any recommendations from store staff on items needed to do a job well.

After researching and taking time to think it over, don't let the lack of a hard list prevent you from walking past the impulse buys.

Rule 7: Use Cash or an Expense Tracking App

Cash is often touted as a way to keep better track of your spending and it can work well for many people. If you're like me, however, everything goes on plastic. I use my debit card almost exclusively to avoid ATM fees. Also, I don't spend as much as I would if I had cash burning a hole in my wallet.

For those who do use cash, it gives you an instant understanding of exactly how much you have and what you're spending. It can be more difficult to hand it over for something you picked up on a whim. Using cash also means change, which can be collected to fund a trip or an experience in your own backyard.

If you're interested in money tracking apps, there are a number out there and many of them free. Some banks even include the service as part of their online banking feature. Whichever app you choose, they all have their own features meant to keep you accountable. Pie charts, notifications, alerts, and plenty of design elements with bright colors keep your mind on your money and help you avoid impulse purchases.

Rule 8: One In One Out

I saved the best rule for last. This rule is key to helping you keep up your practice. It stands on its own as well as acts as a backup if you miss any of the previous rules. When you bring something home, find something else to take out of your home. This allows you to maintain the balance you've worked hard to find and keeps down the clutter.

It's not a crutch for bypassing the rules above. Simply cycling items in and out of your home to maintain a minimalist façade will be fruitless if your consumer habits remain unchanged. Do not fall into the trap of replacing your holiday decor each year because of a good deal or finding a new design more appealing.

The 8 rules above will help you in the shopping process. Whether its everyday shopping at the grocery store or a special trip to a furniture shop several hours away, keep these rules with you to support your practice of minimalism. When it comes to purchasing something new, I have another set of rules to help you.

Buying with Intention

This section is a set of questions to ask yourself about the item or items you'd like to purchase. We covered finding right intentions in the previous section, but these questions are here to help with the practical side of purchasing something new for your home.

Question 1: Is This Item a Need or a Want?

There are many items we see for purchase everyday. Our desires grab at different ones and it's important to distinguish if an item we want fulfills a need or a want. An item that fills a need will typically serve an active purpose. You most likely don't own it already or the item you had that served the purpose is broken. An organizing tray for your bathroom drawer will actively sort and separate bathroom items for ease of access. A new broom with dustpan will actively help keep your home clean. A new decorative plate or figurine collection might not actively serve a purpose and should be considered more carefully.
Or maybe altogether forgotten.

Question 2: Is This Item Something You Love?

An item you love will hold a higher place in your heart and home than one you just picked up for convenience. You may find need for a new broom and dustpan, but you may not love the one that happens to be in the cleaning aisle at the grocery store. Go back to the purchasing section, do your research, and find one you love with the features you need. Loving an item that you purchase will also serve you well as you care for it and put it to good use. A special occasion dress you adored and purchased to replace one that is worn out will benefit from the love you had for it in the dressing room. You'll keep up the proper dry cleaning schedule after wearing and store it lovingly.

Question 3: Where Will This Item Live?

This question should be easy to answer the farther along in your practice. Allowing space in your home for changing needs is a happy side effect of minimalism. Consider the space an item should live in. A new lamp for reading might be obvious, but where should you store sports gear that needs to be accessible throughout the year? Determining where a new item should live may even take some rearranging of your current organization. Take that into consideration and make those moves before you bring your new purchase home. If you live in a small space and need to purchase a larger item, consider alternatives to buying such as renting or using items available for use at a designated place in your neighborhood. On the other hand, you may have committed to a particular exercise routine and would like to bring the equipment into your home. In that case, weigh the positive impact on your health with the setup of your space and make the necessary adjustments.

Question 4: Will You Use It Often?

Continuing the example of new exercise equipment, it's important to honestly assess how much use you will gain from a new item purchased. Someone who is already committed to a cycling class 3 times a week will gain more from owning their own stationary bike than someone who tried a class once, but loved it. When gauging how much you might use something, I suggest trying before you buy. A new kitchen gadget sounds like a useful addition to your home, but could be just another item to store if you don't use it. See if a friend has the model you're looking to buy and try it out. Find your favorite exercises that keep you coming back before bringing home gym equipment.

Keep in mind, however, that whatever you bring home will require its own maintenance, cleaning and storage. That's additional time taken away from other parts of your life.

Question 5: Do You Own Anything With a Similar Purpose?

Oftentimes the needs we have that require a purchase can be met by something we already own. You may have an empty plastic bin that would be perfect for the sweaters you're trying to store. A rarely used lamp in one room can turn into an active source of light by moving It to another room. Carefully consider the items you already own to see if anything would provide a sensible solution to your need.

It goes without saying that you can consider the above for each household member, not just yourself. Oftentimes, when you progress from impulse buying for your own needs, your brain can switch to the needs of others. You see a pair of shoes you know your friend was looking for and they're her size! There's the exact phone case your partner wanted and it's on sale. Even if you're avoiding stores and unsubscribing from retailer emails, these items can find you and grab you.

One household member to keep in mind is the four-legged kind. Cats and dogs are common pets requiring their own set of items to stay healthy. Cats love to play out their hunting instinct with toys and need to keep their nails in check with good scratching surfaces. Dogs need leashes, toys, beds, and more to keep them satisfied. It's important to care for your pets and provide the items they need. Then, avoid unnecessary trips to pet stores. If at first you find it difficult to ignore the calling of the newest chew toy, find a new way to get pet necessities. Several pet and big box web retailers offer subscription services to deliver food, treats, and litter on a set schedule. The service helps you avoid adding extra items to your cart and frees up the time spent going to the pet store. There is more packaging and transportation involved when items are delivered to your house. Consider the needs of your family and if you can transition back at some point in your minimalist practice to pet store shopping.

The tips and rules in this chapter are not meant to restrict you or lessen your excitement about shopping. On the contrary, they're intended to inject more joy into bringing something new into your home. You should bring home items that you're proud of and will help you in your home. You put in time, as well as, effort to find these necessary items, so each one should receive the highest standard of care and shine wherever it lives. By adopting these principles when it comes to shopping and buying new items, you avoid the trap of creating more clutter.

Chapter 3. Living Room

Decluttering Strategies That Will Inspire You

The living room looks different in every home. In smaller homes, it occupies little space in order to share with other rooms and their adjoining functions. In larger homes, there may be formal and casual living rooms that stand on their own. In any scenario, a living room lives up to its name. It's meant to hold the life that goes on in the home. It's often the space where you spend most of your time, outside of the kitchen. It contains space for your family to gather together, including pets. Practicing modern minimalism in the living room can yield the greatest benefit because the open and stress-free space promotes harmony while minimizing conflict. With less physical clutter in the living room, mental space expands while energy increases.

Interior Designer Nate Berkus once exclaimed "In a minimal interior, what you don't do is as important as what you *do* do!" That is to say, those minimal interiors you peruse on Pinterest didn't happen by accident. They're the product of intention and effort. It takes more than white-washing walls and adding in sleek modern furniture. It's about making the physical space for your mental space. In the living room, that means finding the style you want to present yourself and your guests. I've put together practical tips for this chapter to help you remove the physical clutter and open up your space to achieve your minimalist goals.

The Living Room Game Plan: 12 Steps

Before getting started, make sure to remove extraneous objects from your living room. Some items may be better suited to other areas, but many things should be looked at and taken out of your living room completely.

1. Find a Wall Color That Brings Light

White walls reflect light the best and ignite an instant feeling of cleanliness and calm. White is an especially impactful color in the living room because of the many activities that take place there requiring light. It is perfect for reading, working on a puzzle or conversing with a gathering of friends. Having a wall color that reflects light back into the room helps your living room live up to its full potential.

White isn't the only option for your living room. Depending on your design, you can opt for a light color in purple, gray, or yellow hues. If you're going to go with a color other than white, keep that in mind as you put your room back together with furniture and decor. The point is to find what works for your style while still providing a calm background for the room.

2. Keep Decorations Simple

The decor in a living room shouldn't distract from the life that goes on within its walls. It can and should follow a theme that threads together throughout the room. Avoid mixing and clashing styles of items to keep the mental space open. If there's a bookcase, avoid stuffing every shelf full of books. Instead, choose select books that are often used or discussed and place them amongst the shelves. Leave space between clusters of books to break them up aesthetically and avoid overwhelming the shelf.

Other surfaces should remain mostly free to allow for temporary uses. A tray of appetizers or drinks during game night can easily find a place when you don't clutter surfaces with decor. Fireplace mantles or floating shelves are decor elements themselves and can provide additional space to draw attention to particular decor items. In addition to keeping the physical space clear for your mind, you'll find it easier to display holiday decorations.

Practical items like remote controls for TV's or monthly periodicals waiting to be read can find homes on a shelf of a side table, in a basket, or in a drawer in a piece of living room furniture. This keeps them within reach without being part of the decor.

Mixing design styles in the living room to put everything you hold dear on display will distract from those special pieces. By ordering your decor into one theme, you can easily draw attention to your style and the pieces that are important to you.

3. Add Texture

With smooth walls and clear surfaces as a base, you can introduce texture into the room in a variety of ways. Find pillow covers with larger than normal loops in the weave of the fabric. Opt for a velvet couch cover or one with a woven fabric. Find a rug that sits between low pile and shag that's easy to maintain but still offers texture.

You might even forego a color on one wall and pattern it with a removable wallpaper that has texture. In the absence of a textured wall, consider the artwork you'd like to hang and opt for something bold and structured. Texture is a special element to add to your living room exhibiting warmth. It can even enter the room through the light fixtures.

4. Make Special Furniture the Star of the Show

The living room is the place for your statement piece of furniture to shine. The chaise lounge you inherited from a family member. The one-of-kind coffee table made out of walnut with a live edge. The living room can be the launching pad for this prized furniture and stand out amongst the sleeker design elements.

A statement piece of furniture in the living room garners the attention it deserves from the frequent use of the room. Guests can appreciate it more often while you have the pleasure of using it in your everyday life. In order to keep the space open when displaying your piece, minimize decor elements around it. If it's a seat of some sort, keep pillows or blankets to a minimum and simple in design. If it's a coffee table, avoid cluttering it up with magazines or other items. The salvaged mantle with aged wood grain shines best without cluttering it to the point it looks like any other shelf you might have installed.

5. Share Your Style

The living room doesn't have to be devoid of your personal style. Choose an element that defines your personal style and integrate it into the room. If natural color wood is a design element you love and defines your style, add it to the room. Maybe your style is big and bold, like pops of bright color in the decor pieces.

Your living room is an extension of you and should be treated as such when organizing and decorating the space. Tying your personality into the details of the room is part of what makes it a calm and peaceful place. It's what will make friends and family say "Yes, that's you!" when they come to visit.

6. Use Greenery for Softness

Whether you stick with clean lines throughout the space or add in texture, there's always room for some softness, too. Plants are an excellent way to add greenery and a soft element to the room. You can even find plants that specialize in cleaning the air. If you're worried about keeping plants alive, especially while traveling, consider succulents that require less water but still offer the soft texture.

It's easy to add plants without taking up surface space, whether on furniture tops or the floor itself. Simple plant hangers make it easy to add plants without cluttering up the floor. They draw your eye up to see the expanse of the room and when hung at the right height, are easy to keep watered.

7. Make A Difference With Subtle Color

If bold colors are not part of your personal style, consider adding subtle color through items like books, a collectable vase, or even a blanket in the seating area. Staying in the same color family adds visual interest while displaying the items you want those visiting your living room to see.

You can also add color using the softer elements of your design. Curtains, pillows, and even upholstery can carry soft color throughout your room.

8. Embrace the Dramatic

The style and architecture of your home may lend itself to drama in the form of intricate baseboards, door frames and custom built-ins from another era. Whatever elements your home provides, you can play up the drama with items like dark toned curtains or a dramatic color for your couch. The point is, with all the work you've put into organizing and going minimal within the living room, you've now made space for drama.

9. Highlight Your Art

The living room is the perfect place to display your favorite art. Not only will it receive the appreciation of guests, but more admiration from yourself as you spend more time in the space. In a clean and minimal living room, your art can take center stage while other elements remain simple. It doesn't need to take up an entire wall either. If you have a piece or series of pieces that can be framed to match, a mantle or other shelf may be the perfect place to display it.

No matter the media, you can get creative in hanging and displaying. Hidden frame hangers that attach to the wall behind the art may be best for some pieces. For others, displaying elongated wires hanging on nails might fit the design of the room better. Even still, a simple picture shelf hung the length of a couch may be the right fit for the room.

10. Focus On Smaller Decor Elements

Chances are, you're not reading this book to complete a full overhaul of each room in a weekend. The focus is on reducing clutter and while that is achievable in every room, new furniture and decor in every room may not. Don't worry. Take the design elements that are the easiest to change out: paint, curtains, even a slipcover for the couch/chairs and turn them to neutral to contribute to the feel of minimalism in the room.

Your home may have older wood floors in patterns no longer offered or you're still holding onto a retro couch because it's in great condition. Whatever the case, you can find ways to modernize and quiet loud patterns. Find a simple monochromatic rug to cover part of the old floor.

Cover up the bright 90's floral pattern on your couch with a slipcover from the store or your linen closet for an instant calm.

11. Highlight Views or Patterns

If your living room happens to feature an amazing view, run with it. The mountains, trees, or even a city unfurling before you all capture attention and make a great focal point in the room. You can place furniture to take full advantage of the view while minimizing decor around the window or windows.

If you're in an apartment with windows facing other windows or don't like the view out of your living room, get creative. Use patterns in the wall decor to draw the eye to a view of your own creation. A set of black and white photos with matching frames would work perfectly. Or a triptych of a pattern spanning a large section of a wall will garner attention.

12. Bring In the Light!

The living room is used at all hours of the day. Take into consideration the additional light you'll need at night. Also consider the cloudy days and the times when the sun isn't bursting through the windows and doors. You may need a lamp for reading in your favorite chair or lounger. If you lack overhead lighting, consider adding fixtures to the walls in even numbers to add light and keep the design smooth. Wall light fixtures also save floor space keeping the open and calming feel you want for the space. You don't need an electrician, either. Many wall fixtures are wired. With a little paint and hardware, you can affix the wires to the wall and avoid the intrusion of a tangled wire mess.

There's a bonus step that will apply to most homes, but not all. This step calls for you to make space for pets. Cats and dogs require space and even furniture to keep them comfortable. Consider them when planning out the space and take advantage of new furniture designs with more than one purpose. If your living room is small and includes the entryway into your home, consider a bench that conceals a litter box underneath. If you have a strict "no dogs on the couch" policy, find a stylish pet bed in their size to work into the design and flow of the space.

If you have fish or other terrarium-dwelling pets, consider making their home the focal point of the room. Focus on their housing and design to draw attention not only to them, but their stylish habitat. A minimalist living room with pets will look different from a minimalist living room without pets. That's okay, though, because pets provide their own kind of mental benefit and inspire peacefulness with their unconditional love.

These 12 steps will apply differently to each person depending on personal style and taste. It's also important to consider the shape and size of your living room.

This book is for you to make your own and it's up to you to decide what elements work best in your space. These 12 steps are a guideline to help you as you continue to practice modern minimalism. They're a reward in themselves for the hard work you're putting in to make your space the calm and serene retreat you deserve.

Chapter 4. Bedrooms

The Best Kept Secrets to Serenity

The bedroom is a sacred place in the home. It's where you rest and recharge to recover from the outside world. It should be an open space that supports meditation and better sleep. Modern minimalism supports this goal by cutting down on the clutter and turning up the calm. If you start the process with the understanding that the bedroom is the one place in your home to recharge, the rest is easy. I've put together 10 tips to achieving the sanctuary to inspire and rejuvenate. Take note of what is achievable right now and what you can plan for in the coming weeks and months. The bedroom is worth pondering over and planning carefully.

Before we get started with the 10 tips, I wanted to advise on the bedroom-specific clutter often found. Televisions are ever more popular in bedrooms especially as their price goes down and the screen size goes up. They can be distracting in the space, however, and should be relegated to a different room or disposed of altogether. Our laundry often finds its way into all corners of the bedroom. Instead of keeping a laundry hamper or basket in the bedroom, make space for it in the bathroom or closet. These are spaces where you're more likely to get dressed and undressed, anyway. Books and magazines often stack up on bedside tables, even after they've been read. Reading is a soothing part of a bedtime routine and in order to support it and maintain calm, keep the materials to a minimum. Find storage out of sight, in a bedside table drawer or a basket on the shelf of the bedside table. You'll want to keep your reading materials close, but still save surface space from the clutter.

Cash may no longer be king in terms of what you carry in your wallet, but loose change seems to always find its way to the dresser top. Minimize this by designating a place for it out of sight and regularly deposit coins at your bank to keep it from piling up. Jewelry trays that often catch the loose change and jewelry pieces worn that day should be removed and if possible, stored with your clothes in your closet. Consider investing in a low profile alarm clock to use in place of your phone alarm to disconnect further from the outside world. If an old school alarm clock isn't your style, utilize the do not disturb settings on your phone to block all notifications during a set time each night. Landline phones, much like TV's, do a wonderful job of keeping us up. Take care to minimize them in your bedroom sanctuary.

If you have pets, chances are they prefer sleeping in your bedroom with you. Consider them in the design of the space to support their needs. If your dog sleeps in a crate, consider one that can double as a nightstand to save space and add style. Cats often sneak onto your bed but can also prefer a bed of their own. Assess your cat's preference and provide the sleeping setup they need. Make sure your cats have access to their litter box and water, if you close your door at night. Careful consideration of your pets and their needs during the process of decluttering your bedroom prevents imbalance of objects down the road. You don't want to find yourself in the final stages of designing the space only to realize there's a scratching post that now has to find a place to live in the bedroom.

Choose a Calming Color for the Wall

Just like in the living room, start with the basics in your bedroom: wall color. There's a lot of research on the psychology of color and how it affects our moods and psyches. Keep that in mind when choosing a color in your bedroom. A creamy warmer white is always in style and gives you a blank canvas feel. With no distraction of color, your mind can clear itself of thoughts and worries to promote restful sleep.

Blue is another color suited for the bedroom. A lighter shade can perfectly compliment neutral beiges and tans found in other parts of the room. Its effect on your mood is a calming one, but not draining. Seek a shade that doesn't overpower the room with boldness, but one that sits just in the background putting out a constant air of calm.

Pink is the tranquil partner of the color red. It can be suitable for a bedroom in lighter shades that don't overwhelm the design. Dusty pinks can provide the tranquility of the pink family without being overbearing. If you consider this color for your bedroom, make sure to take into account the other elements to prevent color clashing.

Pick Out a Minimal Bed Frame

In order to keep your bed suited to its purpose, which is sleep and sex, consider a minimal bedframe. Trends in furniture design are slowly turning away from the clunky and chunky furniture from even a few years ago. Many retailers from big box stores to established furniture makers offer a selection of minimal bed frames. These pieces feature clean lines and neutral colors so the focus in your bedroom is on you and your rest.

You may also choose to go without a bed frame and utilize a standard metal box spring frame to give you a little elevation off the ground. Without the added element of a bed frame, your bedroom opens up even more and detracts less from its purpose. It can be easier to keep your room clean without a bed frame with no need to dust and cleanliness being just a load of laundry away. Whatever style you choose, carefully consider the size of your room and your sleeping needs when choosing a bed. A king bed in a small room may not make sense unless you're able to balance its size with restricting other bedroom furniture. You might install floating side tables to balance the floor space taken up by a larger bed. You could rely on other furniture being off the ground either with legs or with installation on the wall.

Select Neutral Colored Bedding

Now that you've selected your bed, it's time for soothing bedding. Your bedding needs will depend on the seasons where you live. You may use a top sheet or opt for the European style of just a fitted sheet. Your local climate may require a heavy quilt and comforter for part of the year or a light blanket year-round. Whatever the case, use the opportunity to dress your bed as one to supplement the calm in the bedroom.

One way to do that is with a monochromatic bedding scheme. All white or all beige brings focus not on changing colors from pillowcase to fitted sheet, but to a blank canvas. A blank canvas where your thoughts and dreams are free to roam. Depending on your need to keep clothing and other decor in your bedroom, bedding is a simple way to minimize and open the space.

Thread Neutral Tones Throughout the Room

With neutral bedding in place, continue to thread those tones throughout the room. Rather than have a statement piece of furniture like in the living room, try to keep colors in the same family. This will prevent the room from being overwhelmed with too many focal points. By keeping neutral colors running throughout the room, you're creating an open space for you to recharge. Clutter can come in many forms and color is one of them. Just like you can have too many physical objects, you can have too much color that distracts from the space's true purpose.

This is especially important to keep in mind when organizing your bedroom. Find matching furniture pieces or stain ones to match. Consider the color on your wall before bringing in furniture pieces and keep decor in line with the color and tones you choose.

Find the Right Lighting

Lighting in the bedroom is a delicate art. At night, blackout curtains may be necessary to keep environmental light from waking you. During the day, you want as much natural light as possible to encourage you to use the space for meditation and reflection. Starting with the windows, find treatments that suit your needs while also maintaining the minimal aesthetic. This may look like a double-rod setup to hold a sheer curtain as well as blackout curtains in a neutral color. It could also mean shades or blinds meant to cover the entire window to block out light as needed. Whatever it looks like for you, make sure to keep in line with the other design and color selections you made for the room.

After natural light, the next best lighting in a bedroom is soft warm light emanating from carefully selected and placed light fixtures. LED light bulbs are pretty much ubiquitous nowadays. In the absence of the typical older style light bulbs, LED manufacturers have stepped up with more choices in light tones. It doesn't need to feel stark or sanitary in your room. Look for LED bulbs that say "soft light" or use marketing language like "relax." Better yet, visit a local hardware store to see bulbs on demo and find the one that works for you. There's a perfect hue that allows for relaxation, meditation and calm activities like reading.

Display Artwork

A bedroom is a sanctuary, hallowed in your home. This is a chance to display art that inspires calm and elicits positive feelings. To avoid cluttering the bedroom with art, choose one piece to display. You can always change it out with another piece should you feel the need. By having one piece of art on display, you're contributing to the feeling of open space.

Placement of the art will depend on its medium (sculpture or canvas painting) as well as the setup of the room. If you opted to go without a bed frame, a canvas above your bed that evokes feelings of calm is perfect. If you have a beloved sculpture, a separate pedestal or a space on a dresser free of clutter would give it the recognition it deserves.

Find One Place to Display Mementos

Our bedroom is where we are most vulnerable. When we sleep, we let go of our defenses in order to restore ourselves for the next day. It makes sense to keep the other parts of our vulnerable selves in our bedroom. Black and white photos of relatives, a specially gifted perfume, dried flowers from a special day all hold a sacred place in your heart. It's important to give these items space in your bedroom, without letting them devolve into additional clutter distracting the room from its purpose.

To prevent cluttering of mementos, find one space in your bedroom where you can thoughtfully arranged the pieces that mean the most to you. A low profile floating shelf or a small section of a dresser top could serve this purpose. Carefully select the pieces you want to display and store the rest. You may feel the need to change out what is on display. Keeping these items to a minimum means you can swap out as you see fit.

Add Greenery

Pops of green work well in every room, but live plants in bedrooms are especially beneficial. You're breathing the air in your bedroom all night and even with a clean filter in your central air conditioning system, there's still plenty to be filtered out. Plants provide the benefits of electric air purifiers without sacrificing style and design. Utilizing the natural light in your bedroom, find a place to set up a minimal plant stand or take advantage of hanging options to keep your floor space clear.

While all plants remove CO_2 from the air, there are some in particular that are adept at cleaning the air indoors. Consider a spider plant or a bamboo palm for pure green. Dragon Trees or Chinese Evergreens also keep your air fresh. Visit your local lawn and garden store for suggestions from the experts on your particular area. Even if you have access to plants that require a lot of sun, it may not be the best choice for your climate and even the direction your bedroom windows face.

Choose Your Clothing Storage Wisely

In the absence of a closet that can hold not only all your hanging clothes but the clothes that need to be folded, you will have some clothing storage in your bedroom. In your process of minimizing the amount of clothing you own, you should be able to get the items of clothing down to a manageable level. The next step with turning your bedroom into a sanctuary is choosing the right furniture to store your clothes.

Ideally, you should be able to fit all your clothing into one piece of furniture. A taller chest of drawers takes up less vertical space and can draw the eye up. A shorter chest of drawers with a greater width can offer surface area for the proper lighting and minimalist storage of jewelry. You may need something completely different because of closet space or even the makeup of your wardrobe. You may need an actual wardrobe that has hanging space accompanied by a few drawers for the clothing items that absolutely need to be folded and stored. When you find what works for your needs, think about where it should go in the space to maximize its functionality. Stick with it. Place near a window for maximum light or next to the bathroom door to make dressing easier.

Minimalism Does Not Equal Cold

All of the tips and suggestions in this chapter will make a world of difference in your bedroom. They're exactly what you need to make your bedroom the calm and restful place you deserve. They help you pare down the excess to make room for the possibilities. That is what modern minimalism is about. It's not here to turn your home into a cold prison-like shelter devoid of warmth. It's here to open up your space which allows you to open your mind. You should have warmth in your bedroom and following the tips in this book will get you there.

Putting together your perfect minimalist bedroom is a reward that renews itself with each period of sleep. Your bedroom is an escape from responsibilities and everyday struggles. Your efforts to make the space reach these goals will be felt daily. Take it one step at a time and remember your goals for practicing minimalism. You're on your way to a bedroom and a home of your dreams.

Chapter 5. Laundry Room
The Game Changing Routine You Need

With how often you use the laundry room, it may seem daunting to apply minimalist principles to its organization and function. I argue that because of the high volume of use, it's the easiest room to implement a solid strategy for organization and functionality. The first step is to assess the space. Laundry rooms vary in size and can hold more than one function, such as a back entry to your home with a mudroom. If you're in a smaller space or live in a home designed to maximize square footage to other purposes, you may have little more than a closet. The closet may not even have storage and be completely taken up by machines. Whatever the setup, take a minute to analyze what you're using the room for currently.

Once you have an idea of how you're currently using the space, it's time to learn a new routine. These new habits make the most of the space and allow for you to keep the minimalist mindset you're practicing in the rest of your home. After reading and adopting the following routine, I'll lead you through the reorganization of the space to best suit your needs. Say goodbye to random piles of laundry and spilled laundry detergent. Say hello to clean lines and open space.

Habit 1 - Wash A Load Every Day

One of the biggest factors contributing to messy laundry rooms is a pile of dirty clothes ready to be washed. Allowing clothes to pile up and waiting for a specific day of the week to clean means that laundry day is the only day the room is truly clean. In order to maximize your efforts to create a modern minimalist home, adopt the habit of washing a load of laundry every day. Between sweaty gym clothes, sheets, blankets, and towels, there's plenty to wash on a daily basis. You don't have to be excessive in what you wash; jeans and dry-clean-only clothes typically don't need a wash after one wear.

If you do find yourself with too little to wash each day, consider washing every other day to keep the clutter to a minimum. If you find that many items are too delicate for the dryer, find a permanent setup for drying. Depending on your space, you could install a minimalist rack matching the color of the door to blend in and always be at the ready to dry clothes. You could also use any wall space in your laundry room to affix a simple rack in a neutral color, like natural wood. If wall or door space is not an option, find a smaller than standard folding drying rack that can be set up for the days you have delicates to dry. A smaller sized rack can easily hide between one of the machines or tucked behind a door.

Habit 2 - Don't Overfill with Detergent

If you're using liquid detergent, chances are you're using too much. Detergent formulas are heavily concentrated and using less than what the bottle says will still produce clean clothes. Overusing detergent also runs the risk of leaving residue on your clothes and irritating sensitive skin. Stick to just below the recommended line on the dispense cup and save money and plastic by not going through as many detergent bottles.

While liquid has long overtaken the market, powder is beginning to make a comeback. One of the benefits is its lighter weight and less packaging as compared to standard liquid detergent. Both of these features save on fuel for transport and thus can result in a lower price compared to liquid. In addition to being a bit more friendly to the environment, powdered detergent is much easier to store and keeps with the minimalist aesthetic. You can find a container that fits in with the design of your laundry room and avoid having the bright marketing colors of liquid detergent bottles distracting from a clean space. As a bonus, many manufacturers of powder laundry detergent set out to make formulas with less chemicals. This is a boon to those with sensitive skin and people looking for more natural alternatives to modern detergent ingredients.

Habit 3 - Cold Water is Key

Using cold water in all your wash cycles simplifies your work leaving space for your mind to focus on other things. Cold water not only works for delicates or heavy-duty textiles like towels, it also saves money. By foregoing the hot water, you're using less energy and reaping the benefits on your energy bill each month. Cold water is also excellent for a wide range of stains, including blood, whereas hot water can set those protein-based stains.

If you have greasy or grimy rags from cleaning, simply give them a hot rinse in your sink before throwing them in to wash. Cold water will help all your fabrics last longer and is especially useful for clothes, towels, and bedding. This simple habit dramatically impacts how you do laundry and reduces the costs associated with it.

Habit 4 - Sort By Color No More

Fabric dyes used in modern clothes are more likely to be steadfast and less likely to bleed onto other fabrics in the wash. Take advantage of this aspect of modernity and start sorting your clothes by the type of fabric rather than the color. By dividing clothing and linens by fabric, you streamline the number of loads and the cycle types needed. Most homes will use two cycles: delicates and regular. The difference is in the spin speed and is meant to support the longevity of more delicate pieces.

When you bring new pieces of clothing or other linens into your home, wash them once to test their steadfastness, especially if they're darker colors. A wash will also clean off dangerous manufacturing dust and leftover chemicals.

Habit 5 - No Need for Dryer Sheets

The last habit to adopt is getting rid of dryer sheets. Their benefit as a static remover is overshadowed by the chemicals present in them. Not to mention, the need to replenish stock on a regular basis eats into your wallet. Cut one more thing off your shopping list by getting rid of dryer sheets. If you're looking for an alternative to help with static and fluff up linens like towels, consider wool dryer balls. You can find them at big box stores and natural food stores. Toss a few in the dryer for each cycle and store them in a container that matches your laundry room aesthetic. Wool dryer balls last a long time and you won't have to worry about replacing them as frequently as dryer sheets.

By now, you can see how these habits build on each other. They each have a purpose on their own. Taken together, they're a new routine to streamline the work of your laundry room. By adopting this routine, you will cut down on the mental space devoted to a necessary household chore. This is especially beneficial as laundry is ongoing. The savings in your time, money, and energy stacks up quickly with these new habits.

Now that you've adopted helpful habits in the laundry room, it's time to set up the space to keep you successful in your new routine. I touched on helpful tools and storage ideas in the previous section, but in this one, I want to walk you through every aspect of a laundry room. By thoroughly assessing your needs, you can set up a space that is functional and easy to keep clean.

Step 1: Group Your Clothes

We only have as much laundry as we do clothes. It seems an obvious truth, but it doesn't really set in until you go from owning mounds of clothes to a few capsules of a wardrobe. With less clothing, you wear more and wash less. Rather than piling up a week's worth of clothing from wearing new pieces each day, you're wearing and washing the same items. This means there's no time for them to pile up on the floor or the laundry basket. If you're following the habit of doing a load each day, then you're able to keep the clothing clutter in your laundry room to a minimum.

Depending on where you live, you may have a wardrobe for each season. Grouping these items together either in your drawers, hanging in your closet, or stored in bins will simplify your routine. It will make getting dressed easier as well as helping you keep track of favorite items that are worn often, and thus, washed often.

Step 2: Carve Out Laundry Spots

So far, I've laid out the best habits for washing and drying laundry. But what about the steps that come before and after the wash? They're just as important and require strategic thinking to streamline the operation. It's time to consider the whole routine of laundry, starting with where you keep dirty clothes. Depending on the layout of your house, you might be able to take the dirty laundry you've just worn and deposit it into the laundry room. This is possible due to the rise in popularity of main floor laundry rooms that take advantage of a convenient water source (bathrooms!).

In the absence of laundry located conveniently next to the room where you undress, you'll more than likely have a hamper. If possible, you should try to find either a low profile hamper or make space in a bathroom cabinet for a basket to catch laundry. In either case, make sure it is easy to carry to and from the laundry room. Invest in two baskets or hampers of the same kind. Keep one in the laundry room, making it easy to transport clean clothes back to their home. Use the second basket in your bathroom to place dirty clothes.

After figuring out a way to store and transport dirty laundry efficiently, tackle the post-wash need for folding space. Reserve the counter space in your laundry room for this purpose. This way you can transport not only clean laundry to a dresser or closet, but folded laundry that's ready to be put away. If your laundry room lacks counter space, consider a folding table that's easy to set up. Some ironing board designs maximize surface space and could function as a folding table in addition to an ironing space.

If space is lacking for folding and ironing in your laundry room, consider moving the job to your closet or right in front of your closet. This will allow you to take clothes straight from the laundry room to a designated space where you can fold, iron, and put away. I mentioned a drying rack in the previous part of this chapter and want to bring it up again. If you're short on space, the back of a door or empty wall space would hold a rack perfectly. If that doesn't work in your space, consider a smaller drying rack that's easy to both fold and unfold. The advantage of a smaller rack is that if you do need to use it on a daily basis, it won't take up as much room and leaves more space wherever you set it up.

Step 3: Make the Most of the Space

Part of assessing your laundry room is discovering every area that may contribute to storage and organization. I've already mentioned the back of the door as an option, as well as the wall. With the right bins and containers, you can have everything you need to wash your clothes at the ready. If the door to your washer opens to the left, make sure the detergent is within reach on your right. If your appliances are stacked, take advantage of the additional accessible wall space and floor space to hang cascading baskets. You can keep wool dryer balls at the dryer level and detergent at the washer level. If you have space for closed storage, you can create clean lines and open space with ease.

If your laundry room is really just two appliances stacked to take up every inch of a closet with folding doors, don't worry. Invest in a mini rolling cart with a neutral color that can be organized to hold all your laundry supplies. You can even hook a mini drying rack on one end. With the supplies visible, consider containers to hold supplies that stay true to the theme of minimalism in your home. Containers lined with removable canvas or other fabric are great for accidental spills while opaque jars in varying sizes can hold everything from powder detergent, stain remover and a set of wool dryer balls.

Step 4: Upgrade Your Appliances

Speaking of appliances, consider upgrading the ones you currently have to ones that will better suit your space. If your space allows it, consider a stacking washer and dryer combo that saves on floor space and opens up wall space for built-in storage at your fingertips. Opting for a smaller capacity washer and dryer set helps support your new habit of washing a load each day. Newer washers sense how much water to use, but overall energy use decreases when you downsize your washer and dryer. You don't have to sacrifice the ability to wash bulky things with a smaller capacity set. You can simply separate bulky items like comforters or blankets to wash individually.

Smaller capacity sets tend to come with pedestal drawers. This additional storage space can make even the smallest laundry room more functional by keeping laundry necessities right where you need them. Newer machines will also be the most energy-efficient as standards are exceeded each year by manufacturers. Revel in the ability to lower your energy bills while still keeping your clothing, bedding, and other linens clean.

Step 5: Use Decor to Freshen Your Space

Decor in a room that's usually seen as strictly utilitarian may seem odd, but adding design elements can have a profound impact on the space. I want you to view laundry as not just a necessary evil, but a rewarding chore that can be bolstered along the way. Find a space in your laundry room, a doorway or even a section of the space, that can be divided by curtains. Adding a soft element can balance the hard lines of washers and dryers while serving a purpose as a room divider.

A new coat of paint can also freshen up the area, even if there is not a lot of open wall space. By removing everything from the room and painting a crisp white or even a calming lavender, you're elevating the space. Color can peek out where it can, while offering itself as a positive visual in the space.

Find a new area rug or runner to fit in your space. This will help pick up on loose lint before your next vacuuming, especially if you have hard surface floors in the space. In addition to a rug, add greenery for additional warmth. If your laundry room lacks natural light for plants, consider having two of the same kind to swap out. You can also invest in a high-quality silk plant if you don't want to fuss with switching plants from partial sun to no sun (and back again).

The laundry room is one of the rooms in the home that has a specific job to be performed. Rather than it being a place to live or sleep like the rooms I've already covered, its purpose is to keep the operation of living running smoothly. Efficiency, however, doesn't need to equal utilitarianism. A laundry room can be warm and inviting. It should support you in your chore of keeping the linens in your home clean.

With the proper habits established and the space outfitted to suit your needs, success is right at your fingertips. Enjoy the fruits of your labor with a clean laundry room and an empty hamper each night.

Chapter 6. Kitchen and Dining
Transformative Secrets

The kitchen, much like the laundry room, experiences a near constant flurry of activity. It's used daily and has a lot of accessories and appliances packed into what can sometimes be a very small space. No matter the size, a minimalist kitchen is meant to provide a clean slate every time you step in to prepare a meal or fix a drink. In this chapter, you'll discover ways to store, organize, and declutter your kitchen. With each step you follow, the possibilities of the space unfold before you. Imagine your reorganized kitchen as a space where the flow of activity is natural, items are exactly where they should be, and your mind is cleared of stress.

My kitchen allows me to sink into the therapeutic activity of cooking my favorite recipes and baking my favorite treats. A properly established minimalist kitchen will provide these same therapeutic effects to you. In the first section, I'll take you through the many categories of clutter we all have in our kitchens. In the last section, you'll find practical storage solutions for these categories. Taken together, these sections are transformative.

Step 1 - Declutter Small Appliances

It feels like every year there's a new must-have appliance for your kitchen. Air fryers, pressure cookers, rice cookers, slow cookers and more have found their way onto counters and never left. I am a true believer that no one person or family can make the best use of all the small kitchen appliances cluttering up counter space.

Before tackling the hoard of small appliances cluttering your kitchen, assess their use. Be honest with yourself about how often you use each appliance and how they truly benefit your lifestyle. If you're committed to early morning gym sessions and rely on your blender to give you the nutrients you need, keep it. If the rice cooker you bought after a trip to Hawaii inspired you to make rice at home, but now sits neglected, get rid of it.

The latest small appliances promise all sorts of new features to save you time and cook (mostly) healthy meals. Before considering a purchase, plan out how you would integrate an appliance into your kitchen routine. You can also apply this mindset to appliances you already have, but don't use. If there's one that tugs at you and seems like it would help you, try it out. Fit it into your kitchen routine for a week and see how it goes. If you don't use it at least half the time you prepare food in your kitchen, it's time to let it go.

Microwaves and toaster ovens are some of the most common small appliances. There are benefits to both, but I have found the benefits of a toaster oven outweighing those of a microwave. Microwaves distribute heat in a way that can leave your food flat or curdled (like eggs!). Toaster ovens take the power of a full-size oven and distill it into a smaller area. It can warm up food quickly, without dissolving its texture. Save on the electric bill by using a toaster oven and ditch the microwave.

Step 2 - Stick to One Set of Dishes

I see it on wedding registries of friends all the time. They pick out a 5-piece place setting for an everyday set of dishware and then want 12 or 16 sets! Inevitably, they never have a dinner party that big. If they do, it's way more than 12 people and requires paper or plastic ware to serve everyone. Keeping one set of dishes helps you avoid having the weight of unused items on your mind. Hold onto enough plates, bowls, silverware, and glasses for each member of the household, plus a few extra for guests. The extras are helpful, too, in case you break any in you original set.

By allowing only what you need to serve your household, you're helping boost the habit of washing dishes as you use them. This keeps your sink clean and keeps your dishwasher always ready for its next load.

I wanted to mention all of the miscellaneous dishware that can pile up when you're not looking. Travel coffee mugs, reusable water bottles, lids, straws, and more can end up cluttering your cabinets and not serving their best purpose. Assess your lifestyle and decide if you really need all of these accessory items around. A reusable water bottle is a must-have for me and I recommend keeping one on hand to use daily. Having it closeby helps you stay hydrated and healthy. If you lose it or leave it behind somewhere, you can always purchase a new one if you need to. Travel coffee mugs seem to be in every kitchen. However, if you're not on a long commute in the morning that where it is a necessity, you probably don't need them.

Knives are crucial to eating as well as cooking, but they should be selected for your kitchen with care. A good cook can get away with a lot using just a good quality chef knife. A paring knife is helpful for smaller foods like fruits. If you're feeding a larger family and have bigger cuts of meat in your recipes, a good quality carving knife is also important. If you tend to eat steak often, then a few steak knives would be appropriate. With having less knives, you can invest in better quality versions that will last and make food prep easier. As with each section of items in your kitchen, be honest with yourself about your lifestyle and the needs that go with it.

Step 3 - Keep Only Pans You Use

Retailers make it easy to come home with too many pans by packing up an array of various-sized cookware into one box for one low price. Chances are you won't be cooking meals that require that many different pans and in those quantities. A good retailer has high-quality cookware available for sale individually. Approach what you have currently with an individual mindset to pare down to exactly what you need.

To cook pretty much anything, build a small collection. This includes one omelette pan (between 10 and 12 inches), two saucepans (one large and one small), a stockpot, a strainer and a few lids. Any additional cookware should be kept or purchased only if it fits with your lifestyle. If the only way you eat vegetables is if they're steamed, only purchase the insert for one of your saucepans. If you use a cast iron skillet for sauteing food, simmering soup, or cooking steaks, use that in place of the traditional omelette pan. Some cooks swear by their dutch oven. If that's you, don't worry about the traditional stockpot. The point is to have just what you need and nothing you don't.

Step 4 - Limit Kitchen Tools and Gadgets

Kitchen utensils like spatulas and serving spoons are some of the most common counter clutter. When stored in drawers, they often shift around due to their unique shapes. when packed too tightly, they get stuck in the drawer. I advocate for as few utensils as possible to make your kitchen functional. This means a spatula, one slotted spoon, one soup spoon, one baking spatula, and a whisk. These utensils cover everything from cooking dinner to baking a cake.

Other tools like electric meat carvers or basting brushes are niche products that will only fit in if your lifestyle includes those methods of cooking. If you've been through a phase of making pastry and haven't touched the basting brush since, get rid of it. Make space for only what you do now in the kitchen.

Step 5 - Don't Overstock Food

Between membership warehouse stores to deep discounts on staples at the grocery store, it can be tempting to fill up the fridge or pantry with the deals we find. It's too easy to overstock when shopping for food because it's a necessity. It's easy to tell yourself you should stock up on soup because it's 10 for $10 because you feel you're going to eat it all eventually. But applying that logic to everything in the grocery store, leads to an overload of food. Before you know it, those snacks and boxed dinners are expiring because you never got around to eating them.

Use a membership warehouse to mainly purchase cleaning supplies, paper goods and plastic goods (like garbage bags). Try to only purchase food that you will eat within the week. This often means prepared meals, which saves time and is cost effective. At the regular grocery store, take advantage of the deals on food you consume regularly, but only buy what you need. I have found that the items I love buying go on sale on a regular basis. It doesn't make sense to stock up when another sale is just around the corner. By doing so, you're much more likely to be out or almost out of the food by the time the sale begins again. Compare this to just continually adding to the stockpile every time your favorite foods drop in price.

A good rule of thumb is to stock up on dry goods and shelf food, enough for a month, and then buy fresh ingredients weekly. Even better, purchase fresh ingredients every few days for your recipes. This ensures produce never goes bad and that you have enough of ingredients with a shorter life span (like dairy products). Grocery shopping every few days is not always feasible if the store is out of the way or your schedule makes it difficult to go on a 20 minute stop. However, for the support of minimalism, it is still a good goal to keep in mind

Step 6 - Clear Your Counters

Clean sightlines in a kitchen are instantly relaxing. Without the break in your line of sight caused by an appliance or dish rack, your mind stays focused on the tasks and day ahead of you. Rather than making the kitchen feel cold and unused, clearing as much as possible from the counters gives you a blank canvas. Whatever you decided to cook or bake is not limited by your prep space anymore. It's also easier to keep your counters clean if there are little to no obstacles to move when wiping them down. A clean kitchen starts with counters and when those are clear, you feel motivated to use the space. You immediately feel excited to transform a few ingredients into something spectacular.

I'll go over storage solutions in the next section, but start imagining the shift in your kitchen from moving things off the counter to a better space.

Step 7 - Make Visual Space

There are places in your kitchen where you may not be able to achieve a clear sightline. You need a helpful principle to apply throughout the cabinets and countertops. In this regard, it is best to leave open space between things not only for the modernist look, but for the modernist feeling. Being able to clearly see between items stacked in your cabinet or displayed on your counter makes the space feel bigger. That feeling is also absorbed in your mind. If your mind is seeing less clutter, then it *feels* less cluttered.

Step 8 - Find the Flow of Your Kitchen

If you're lucky, you have the perfect triangle. A perfect triangle is one that is drawn between the placements of the fridge, stove, sink. When those three stations are set up in such a way, you flow between them easily as you prepare, cook, and clean up. Most kitchens possess a triangle. This is the basis of your kitchen flow.

After that, the patterns in the kitchen often rely on the personality and habits of the household members. Find how you flow in your kitchen throughout the day. Start with making your first cup of coffee or tea in the morning and track your movements throughout the day. Over the course of a few days, you'll discover the pinch points in your kitchen. The places where things just don't work as well and should be changed. The coffee supplies are above the coffee maker, but that cabinet is right next to the stove which is really where you need the spices.

Consider the layout of the permanent fixtures of the space, like the triangle, and build stations around that. A prep station could have knives, cutting boards, mixing bowls all within reach while standing in one spot. A breakfast station could be right next to the fridge to make it easy to access juices and dairy (or non-dairy) products while assembling your non-refrigerated breakfast items.

Before we get into the second part of this chapter on the dining room, I want to share some practical storage solutions for the kitchen. These will help you clear your counters and simplify your cabinet storage.

Dry Goods and Other Shelf Food

If you're practicing dividing your kitchen into stations, think about grouping food or other shelf items together with their stations. Bread can be close to the toaster. Coffee and tea can be close to the french press or tea kettle. For all other foods, choose a cabinet or utilize the pantry to organize foods by group. Beans, rice, and pasta should go together. Jars and cans used for making pasta sauce should also be grouped in their own area. By grouping similar items, you're able to clearly see the stock you have and choose what you want based on the variety at hand.

Following the step laid out in the previous section, leave space between groups so you're not overwhelmed when you open the cabinet doors.

Knives

High-quality knives should not be in crowded drawers or in knife blocks. The best storage to maximize their longevity is a drawer with a non-slip pad for each knife to rest on separated from each other. Another alternative is installing a magnet bar on the inside of a cabinet door close to your prep area. This keeps knives safe and in reach when you need them.

Other Cutlery

Find a drawer close to the dishwasher or dish rack and use a divided organizer with non-slip silicone on the bottom, as well as inside the sections. This will keep the set of silverware from moving within the drawer. It will also keep the individual pieces stacked together with space between your forks, spoons, and knives.

Dishes and Glasses

When selecting the cabinet for dishes and glasses, you should consider where clean dishes are distributed from. Separate glasses from dishes to allow easy access to clean plates. If you have a variation in size of glasses, separate those again, but in the same cabinet. By grouping the sizes of glasses together you're making space between them and making it easy to identify what you need when opening the cabinet door.

Coffee and Tea Supplies

Group coffee, tea, mugs, and any accessories together for ease of use. If you keep favorite types of tea or coffee on hand, consider airtight containers to store them in. Immediately get rid of the original packaging. This helps make it easy to access your favorites and continue the minimalist theme in your storage solution. A cabinet would work well for these items. You can adjust shelves to different heights to be able to accommodate everything behind closed cabinet doors. This excludes a large coffee maker, which is best to remain stationed on the counter if used daily.

Kitchen Tools and Gadgets

Avoid keeping tools and gadgets stored on the counter. In addition to creating clutter, you're also exposing the clean tools to the dust in the air. Find a drawer where you can lay out a non-skid pad and set each tool in its own spot with space between. This way everything will stay in place each time you open the drawer and you can easily access the utensils.

Spices and Oils

Store these items close to the stove or prep area where they're often used. If you're using a cabinet to store them, consider step shelves to store spice jars on separate tiers. This makes it easy to spot what you need to use and keeps each jar in its place. Depending on your style of cooking, you most likely just need to have olive oil on hand. It does well in high heat, can add flavor to your food, and is often recommended for health benefits. Keep it close to the stove where you can easily access it when you're cooking.

Pots and Pans

Utilize the width and depth of under the counter cabinets to store your pans using their interior cabinet drawers. One drawer can hold pans while another can store lids. With only the pans you use on a regular basis, it's easy to fit them all into a single cabinet. This is more efficient than the two or more cabinets needed for larger collections.

Dining Room

A dining room is meant for gathering people and food. This space is meant to engage in shared experiences, as well, as creating new memories. A modern minimalist dining room supports that function through clean lines and open space. This allows the conversation and the company to fill the room, unobstructed by clutter. Below are 6 ways to usher your dining room into its next era.

Make Use of Large Open Space

Having a sizable open space for your dining room makes it easier to create the minimalist feel. It allows you to add necessary elements to the room without overwhelming the space. Emphasize the light flowing in from the windows and how it illuminates the space. Align the head of the table with the window. Draw the eye up to the high ceilings. All of these elements bring the peace and calm of modern minimalist design and organization.

In the absence of a large dining room, focus on elements that you can change to make it feel bigger. Adjust the height of the lighting if it hangs low so it's not in your immediate sightline. Consider purchasing a smaller table that can expand if you're a frequent host. Forego other dining room furniture like buffet tables or sideboards to keep the flow of the space clear and open. If you need these items, consider smaller versions that take up less space.

Neutral Colors

With wood being an oft-used material for dining room tables and chairs, you already have a great base for a neutral color palette in the space. Use browns, white, gray, and black to create an enlightening space instead of a distracting one. Decide if you want to thread the same color through all the major elements of the room or mix them.

If you decide to use a few colors, consider the combinations that work best together. An all white room is the epitome of clean and open. You may prefer to balance that, however, with infusions of black. This creates contrast and may make you feel less like you've created a void in your dining room.

Brown and white also balances well. If you have a dark brown wooden table and chairs, consider white seat pads, white walls, and a white sideboard to make the table the star. Lighter color wood, or furniture collections left in their natural state, also pairs well with white. Consider the trim on chairs or adding artwork to bring in this natural color to a white room.

Gray, especially lighter shades, can balance a white dining room or be the base as the color on the wall. You can even make it the focal point with a statement table made with a concrete top. Also consider gray accessories or art to balance with white. Blue can also work in your dining room either as a wall color or in the accessories and decor. Find the color that works best for your room and fits in the rest of your house. There are many options to suit your space.

The Right Lighting

Dining room lighting falls somewhere between bedroom lighting and kitchen lighting. You want to be able to see what you're eating and who you're with, but don't want to set a stark mood with too much light. An overhead fixture should provide ample soft light to create a special feeling while also allowing you to see what's on your plate. Accessory lighting could be wall mounted to emphasize a piece of art or simply highlight the height of the room.

For an overhead fixture centered over the table, consider hanging a little more above the sightline from a seated position. It would be higher than what you normally see in dining rooms, but would allow you to have a clear sightline from a standing and seated position as well as one from a seated position. If you're balancing the amount of light coming from this fixture, the added height should not interfere with the fixture's ability to illuminate properly

Functional Furniture

I mentioned tables with removable leaves in another section and want to highlight here as a perfect example of functional furniture. The ability to accommodate more than just the members of the household is important. You may be hosting a large family dinner or simply adding one more for a casual Saturday afternoon meal. Furniture design has offered this functionality for quite some time, but now there are more options in this realm. Dining tables now come with the ability to expand without having to detach a section of the table and find somewhere to store it. This supports your practice of modern minimalism by removing one more thing from the storage space in your home.

For the purpose of continuity, make sure to have additional matching chairs for your dining table. Attractive folding chairs now come in all styles. If you're storing them for most of the time to keep the minimal feel in the dining space, consider folding chairs instead of standard ones. Sideboards and buffet tables should provide storage to keep linens and candle accessories out of sight when not in use. Designs featuring clean lines and even hidden cabinet pulls will help maintain the minimal feel of the space.

Accent Walls

If you're keeping the contrast between colors to a minimum and have simply-designed furniture, consider an accent wall to spark your dining room. Taking a color from the neutral palette and making one wall stand in contrast to the others provides a backdrop to the furniture.

Use Patterns and Textures

Patterns and textures inject the room with warmth. Play with it by covering seat cushions in a pattern fabric or hanging a tapestry art piece on the wall. Find the places where you can add texture without overwhelming the space. A heavy velvet curtain could adorn either side of the windows. The food you're eating has texture, your dining room should, too.

There's a lot of information in this chapter and you'll see it is one of the longer ones in the book. Its length matches the importance of these two rooms. The place where we cook and the place where we eat are both worthy of great detail. Taking steps to declutter your kitchen will allow you to flourish within it.

By attaining a minimalist look in your dining room, you're opening the space to memories made while sharing meals with friends and loved ones. These rooms require careful thought and planning for all that they contain. The payoff, however, is felt everyday as you utilize both spaces.

Chapter 7. Minimalist Home Office
Essential Hacks

According to the Bureau of Labor and Statistics, the U.S. averaged 8.5 hours of work during the week. The 40-hour workweek is almost a dream at this point. With constant connection through smart phones and home offices, our work is integrated into our lives in new ways. How to make the most of that time can be difficult to determine. In this chapter, I'll walk you through the ways in which a modern minimalist home office supports productivity and help you organize the space to maximize focus.

The most productive minimalist home office has 3 things in common. There is less choice, less tools, and less friction. I'll share more detail below, but first I want you to imagine the more abstract concept of each quality. They all contribute to a more peaceful mind and they're qualities you wouldn't necessarily expect in an office. You may wonder what "less choice" has to do with productivity and how you're supposed to do your job with less tools. Step back and imagine working within a space that combines all 3. Imagine yourself less frustrated by choice, less encumbered by miscellaneous clutter, and how that supports ease of movement both physically and mentally.

Less Choice

The concept of having fewer choices in an office may not be the first thing you associate with a minimalist lifestyle. It's easy to build up an office as a space of infinite possibilities and creativity without end. It is thought of as inspiring and motivating to associate the space where you work with such concepts. Practicing modern minimalism, however, shows how building a space suited to focus rather than chaos helps achieve the dreams and possibilities. It's often said that the most creative people have messy desks and workspaces. Assigning that kind of clutter to every person in search of creativity is like assigning a 4-hour sleep schedule to everyone because that's how Martha Stewart or Jeff Bezos function. Practicing minimalism in your office helps you tap into the creativity by putting down the minimalist organizing methods as a foundation.

In practice, less choice begins with a mental shift when it comes to your work. It's easy to be overwhelmed by the tasks and priorities stacking up in your inbox as well as your mind. Make the choice to focus on what you can control in order to foster productivity. You control how you approach your work and the pattern you follow to complete it. Take a look outside of your work, as well. Identify areas where you can simplify your choices in order to avoid spending time deciding on something. Your home is one place and the work you're doing by reading and applying the principles in this book will lighten the load of choice. Even the simple act of downsizing the amount of cookware in you kitchen creates a few less choices when you open up the cabinet doors.

Even decisions like what to eat and drink are choices drawing on your brain power. Find the routines that take having to decide out of the equation. Find your favorite coffee or tea and stick with that. Plan out your meals for the week concentrating your decision making to one block of time instead of 3 blocks of time every day (plus snacks!). Even your closet is full of decisions to be made. A work uniform would help minimize choice in this area of your life. There's a reason famous CEO's and even regular people who are extremely busy choose to wear the same clothing or same category of clothing each day. They're minimizing choice in the face of all the other important decisions they need to make. Give yourself that same respect.

I encourage streamlining the daily decisions you have to make, but I am not advocating a vanilla lifestyle. Keep your going out dresses and your favorite seasonal drink on deck. You'll need them on the days you set aside for yourself to just focus on you and your family. Taking time away from work is just as important as taking time *to* work. Give yourself space on specific days, to minimize time spent deciding when to have those days to yourself each week. There will be days when the amount of work you've been putting in is wearing on you. Recognize when you're in that phase of work and do what you can to take a mental health day. A spontaneous break from the grind where your decision making is focused on getting a manicure or a massage. Work decisions are not to be made on this day.

Less Tools

I'm going to say something that almost every productivity blog, article, and book out there refuses to admit: forget tools, focus on the work. Forget the best messaging app for small teams, large teams, and in between teams. Forget the best time tracking system or the best timing method to help you focus. Forget the best email suite for communication, the newest laptop, or the latest and greatest phone. In the process of acquiring, learning, and integrating all of these tools, you lose time and energy that could have been devoted to work.

I've tried everything out there to manage projects, communicate with my team, and help me focus on my work. I always come back to simple pen and paper. A written to-do list has always provided a simple way to keep track of tasks and log information needed to keep team members up to date. Combined with a calendar, it's been a boon to productivity and is simple enough to keep me focused on work, not updating a Gantt chart. The problem with the many available productivity hacks is that they require a sort of start up period wherein you're taking time that could be devoted to work and spending it on integrating your style of work into this one box. New hacks are constantly appearing garnering attention and making you question if that would be a better system than what you use now. Productivity hacks will always stay one step ahead of your current system. By relying so much on a productivity tool, you'll be drawn in to whatever bigger and better system comes along.

The same logic applies to technology that is meant to make our work lives better and increase productivity. Sleek advertisements for the latest laptop spark dreams of increased productivity and even better work delivered. But only if you buy it. Your own success can fuel the desire to upgrade your work technology because you deserve it. But be careful. Like productivity hacks, work technology will always stay one step ahead of you. There's always a new version of a laptop or phone on the horizon. You can never really stay on top of it unless you're constantly thinking and deciding on the newest technology to acquire. Don't waste your precious time and mental energy on something that will provide minimal returns at best. With proper maintenance and software upgrades, computers and phones can last longer and provide you with everything you need to do your job well. Don't crowd your mind with anything frivolous. Keep what you have and utilize it to suit your needs. It ultimately saves you money and prevents you from spending your mental energy on something unworthy.

Less Friction

This section could also be called "Less Interruptions" because it is all about minimizing those tiny distractions that pull our brains out of the work. A study from the University of California Irvine followed workers on the job to measure distractions and the impact on their work. What they found is that it takes an average of 23 minutes and 15 seconds to get back on task after a distraction. Multiply that by even a few distractions a day and you're already approaching an hour of work lost each day. An unexpected phone call, a delivery person at your door, or your dog getting into trouble in the house are just a few distractions taking you away from a task.

After that, there's the dozens of notifications received on your phone and desktop pop ups. Each one refocuses your brain, even if it's just information to process and not send a response.

In your office, it's crucial to confront the friction that makes working more difficult.

Remove the desktop pop ups that are often installed when a web page asks you to enable them. Social media sites and email suites are notorious for these pop ups, but your favorite news site is also a source of constant contact. Keep only the tabs and windows open needed to complete the current task. When you're finished with one task, reassess what's open and adjust to set yourself up for the next item on your to-do list.

For your phone, remove email and social media apps completely. Save yourself from the notifications and the irresistible urge to scroll through your feeds. I urge you to try this for one week and see how you do. You'll more than likely find that you missed out on nothing important by keeping these apps off your phone and thus out of your work. If you try it and can't find satisfaction in their absence, there is another option. Go into the settings of each app that sends you notifications. For each one, turn off the notifications. In doing so, you're removing the initial distraction, the ping or vibration of your phone. This allows you to make a conscious choice during intentional breaks to check the apps and review the information you need to know in your email.

Intentional breaks are a crucial part of your workflow. They are the parts of your workday that open your mind and allow it to breathe. Clearing your mind on a walk or scheduled time to take your dog outside to relieve themselves is just as important as buckling down and getting through a task. Take a few minutes and listen to a new album you're excited about. Close your eyes and meditate for 15 or 20 minutes. Refill your water and hydrate. Make yourself a snack and savor it as you eat. Take a step outside of work so you can return with a clear mind and ready to focus on the next task.

At the beginning of this section I took every productivity hack to task. I wanted you to get your mind off of those disruptive "hacks" and onto your actual work. In doing so, you can start to build a simple system that helps you stay organized. I advocate for a to-do list. The best and simplest way to organize it is by week. The likelihood that you will finish a to-do list made for a specific day is very low. Save yourself some time by dedicating one block of time each week to make a list of tasks that need to be done at some point in the week. With less distractions from other sources, your brain will help you decide what is a priority. Spreading it out over the course of the week not only saves you from spending time every day on a list, but helps you feel more accomplished. It can be disheartening to have to carry something over day after day. In this situation, it is also easy to forget your triumphs.

<u>A quick note about project management apps</u>:

> Your organization is likely to use some manner of project management software to help keep teams informed on departmental and cross-departmental projects. You will need to participate, but not to the point where you spend all your time on it. Keep your simple to-do list. Include the task of updating projects on it so your team knows where you stand with the piece of the puzzle assigned to you.

The first part of this chapter got you out of your head and into a new understanding of your office space. The second part will take you through the practical tips to apply when organizing the office space in your home. If you don't work from home or have a side job that you run from a home office space, take these tips with you wherever you work. You may not be able to choose your furniture style or control all the lighting choices, but applying what you can will have a positive impact on your work. I've put together 5 steps to organizing a home office to fulfill your minimalist dreams.

Step 1: Get Rid Of The Clutter

Every time I step into an office supplies store I am taken by the shiny new desk organizers and tools. Matching staplers and pencil cups are (almost) irresistible. They are also unnecessary. In a modern home office, you need much less in the way of physical supplies than you ever did. A whole cup of pens, pencils, and highlighters are unnecessary. Keeping one pen or pencil at hand is enough for your writing needs. Staplers, three-hole punches, and tape dispensers are also just more clutter that most home offices don't need.

Start with the desktop and find the pieces that you don't use. It may seem as though everything is necessary in an office because there is a cultural idea of what encompasses a proper desk. The matching desk accessories at office supply stores are proof of that theory. Forget what is standard fare for a desktop and think about your work. Most work is conducted over the computer and bypasses paper. This in turn cuts the need for paperclips, staples, tape, highlighters, and more.

Move onto the drawers and get rid of anything you don't use on a daily basis. The unused sticky notes and notepads can be recycled. When you need a new notebook or pad of paper for to-do lists, buy one (and only one). The ruler you've had since college, the scientific calculator from the same era, the broken label maker. These should all go. It's easy to carry so much in the way of office supplies because you place a value on it providing you value in the future. Modern minimalism isn't about finding solutions to your future, it's about giving you the space to focus on the now and be ready for what's to come.

Comb through your shelves and bookcases to find the books, notebooks, and binders that are no longer needed. For books, unless you reference the information on a daily or weekly basis, they are not supporting you anymore. If you need a specific book again in the future, you can find it in an electronic version (often cheaper) or through digital rental from your local library (the cheapest). For old notebooks filled with thoughts, ideas, and work notes, decide what is still useful. If you need information to put together a portfolio, create a project for yourself and follow through. Once you've gleaned the information you need from the notebooks, discard them. Keep recent notebooks that you may need to reference in performance reviews and team meetings. If you're keeping work information in binders, periodically go through and see what is still relevant. Consider a more minimalist storage solution for these papers if you are not accessing them on a daily or weekly basis. A paper box in a neutral color or hanging file storage container with a lid also in a neutral color are two good options.

Your home office is the most likely place to keep papers like passports, birth certificates, mortgage papers, and tax info. Here's the best way to store what you should keep. The most sensitive documents, like wills and birth certificates should be in a safe. Any paperwork related to debt such as mortgage origination documents should be kept until the debt is paid off. Tax papers need to be kept for 7 years, an IRS standard. They can be stored in hanging files to make the best use of container space. Seek out a neutral color and matching file storage boxes to keep the look in line with minimalism.

Papers like statements, receipts, or bills that you can get online should not be kept. Set up paperless statements and billing with your bank as well as your credit card company. Manuals to appliances or other consumer purchases are often easily found online allowing you to get rid of the paper versions. Digitize as much as you can, scan papers into your computer and sort them into folders. Take pictures of the documents in your safe to have a backup version. Pictures are not a complete replacement for a document, but may help in your quest to get one reissued.

Step 2: Make Room For Your Space

If your home office is where you conduct the majority of your work, don't skimp on the location in your home. A room or space with lots of natural light keeps you inspired throughout the day and gives you the opportunity for the sun to tell you the (general) time. Whether you have a room with a door to close or a section of an open room to call your office, define it and distinguish it from the rest of your home. Coordinate the color of your desk with the shelving you use to keep essential work tools. Use an area rug to mark the space and bring textured warmth.

By defining your home office with design or architecture, you're preventing the space from becoming cluttered with other uses. It can make sense to use a space big enough for more than one purpose. However, you don't want your office to become a magnet for everything that doesn't have a defined space. Keep your yoga mats and craft supplies somewhere else. You can consider how the space might be made for more than one purpose, but start with the office first. Then you can move on to integrating other needs into the space using minimalist storage and proper placement of furniture.

Step 3: Make A System For Paper

Paper finds its way into our lives on a daily basis. You might need to print something to work on physically. Walking to the mailbox each day brings in half a dozen or more pieces of paper. Make a system to deal with incoming paper to avoid repeating the step of decluttering on a more regular basis. The first action you can take is writing or emailing to the companies and organizations that send you mail. If its credit card offers or charity fundraisers that you give to no matter how much paper they send, reach out and ask to be taken off their list. This will significantly cut down the flow of paper from your mailbox to your desk.

Second, invest in a small minimal paper shredder to keep by your desk. A shredder will keep your work flowing by taking in even nonsensitive papers and collating the shreds into one bin of recycling. If a shredder is too much space, opt for a small profile recycling bin so you can easily recycle papers without having to leave your office.

Third, file important papers immediately. If you're completely converted to digital, scan it in using a scanner or even better, your phone. There are plenty of apps available for free that will take your digital image and convert it into a document to save.

Step 4: Get Rid Of The Extra

Take on the extra decor and furniture in the room to open the space and give it a clean feel. Diplomas, fancy business card holders, awards, and other office decor items should be stored out of sight or removed from the house. Clear shelves and bookcases of these items to leave space next to the books and storage boxes you've put together.

Clear the walls of anything that's distracting. Keep only what is helpful, such as a mirror to check yourself before a video call or a framed print of a quote that keeps you motivated. Even too many good things can be distracting. Be discerning in what you place on your walls and keep in mind the positive effects that open space has on your brain. You want to keep your mind clear while you work and clean walls support that goal.

Assess the furniture in the space and get rid of anything that doesn't belong in an office or is not helpful for getting your work done. This means goodbye to the hand-me-down easy chair that begs to be napped in everyday around 2:00 p.m. Move this furniture to a better place in your home or get rid of it altogether.

Step 5: Set Up Your Desktop

With all the effort put into removing items that don't support your work, the last thing you want to do is counteract that with a messy desktop. Set ground rules for what can be on your desk at any given time. The most important rule to adopt is only keep items on your desk that you are currently using to work. This is not a place to store things and should not be treated as such. Your efforts to clean out drawers and shelves now present an opportunity to store items that are used on a rotational basis. If you don't have drawers, utilize shelves and minimal storage containers to keep these items.

If your work requires you to oscillate between computer tasks and paper tasks that take up the entire desktop, consider how to maximize surface area. Find a drawer to keep your laptop, keyboard, and mouse when not in use. If you have a desktop computer, invest in monitor stands that affix them to the wall. This leaves usable space underneath and allows you to set the monitor at eye level for comfort throughout the day.

Keeping the top of your desk clean is an ongoing effort. You should aim to deal with whatever lands on your desk when you receive it. That may not always be possible. In cases like these, it's helpful to designate a drawer or box on your desk to catch the things that pile up. Be sure to sort through it on a regular basis to keep it from getting out of hand.

A modern minimalist home office is not just about continuing the practice of minimalism in another room of your home. It is a crucial application that supports your mental well-being by supporting your work. It facilitates productivity with simplicity, reduced distraction, and a clean environment. Your minimalist home office is a supporter of professional growth and a gain in mental clarity. Refer back to this chapter often. Work is not a static state but one of constant changes. Keep rooted in the principles and steps laid out in this chapter to support yourself long term.

Chapter 8. Minimalist Storage

The Secrets to Joy in Efficiency

Clothes Closet - Love Everything You See

Your clothes closet may be intended just for clothing, but they're often taken up by other clutter as well. Couple that with how quickly new clothes can pile up on hangers and you're facing a closet disaster. You can never find your favorite top, items become buried for months in the chaos, and you dread putting clean clothes away. The goal of a minimalist closet is to prevent all of the above. It's about decluttering, but also about how you organize what you keep and what steps are needed to support a calm minimalist space. This chapter is for every closet. You may have a grand walk-in closet with high ceilings or an alcove with a door and a hanging rod. Many people live with just a freestanding armoire or similar clothes-hanging furniture piece. Your closet may be unique, but practicing modern minimalism in this space of your home is universal. Combined with the buying and shopping habits in the second chapter, the following steps give you a closet you love to open every morning.

Find Low-Hanging Fruit: Damaged Clothing

The items that are no longer in wearable condition provide an easy entry point into organizing your entire closet. They're low hanging fruit because they are no longer functional. They're objectively unwearable and don't necessarily have the same emotional effect on you as the top you bought last week or your grandmother's wedding dress.

I put this step first so you can practice going through your closet with an easy search filter. File through all your clothing and pick out each one that is stained, ripped, faded, or broken. You're likely to have a good idea of these pieces before you start, so this step will go quickly. By removing these pieces, you also begin to open up space in your closet for the next steps in organizing.

Mid-Hanging Fruit: Clothes That Don't Fit

This step is only slightly more difficult, but easier to tackle after completing the first step. Get rid of the clothes that don't fit. You may have tried on a piece at the store and found when you got home it just doesn't fit correctly. There are pieces that are too big or too small that you thought could work anyway. There are pieces that fit but were never really your style and have stayed on the hanger since you brought them home. Whatever the case, they are weighing on you and need to be gone.

In addition to taking up space in your closet, they're taking up space in your mind each time you see them in the closet and wonder why it is you can't wear them. They can spark questions of "Why can't I pull that off?" or "If only I could lose/gain 10 pounds." These thoughts and questions are part of what modern minimalism is working against. This mental clutter is draining and unsupportive of a meditative peaceful life. Your home should be a safe place and by removing triggers of negative thoughts you can support that goal. Save your mental space for more important things. Take comfort knowing the clothes that you take from your closet can be given away to benefit someone else.

Buck the Trends

As you're going through your closet, you're apt to find pieces bought based on trend and less on enduring quality and style. Reassess retaining trendy pieces in your closet to avoid ending up with out-of-style clothing when the next trend sweeps in. Remember to take a minute to understand how these trends end up in your closet. The fashion industry, and especially fast-fashion retailers, constantly change the course of style to keep consumers coming back. If they all just focused on classic styles with quality materials, consumers wouldn't need to buy as many clothes as often.

Knowing that, take time to look at the clothing you do have and the favorite pieces that spend very little time on a hanger. Start to put together your own style and look. Find the pieces that go together well and make you feel wonderfully confident. Lean into it and build what you have in your closet around that look. In addition to the positivity radiating from confidence in your wardrobe, you can shop for new pieces knowing exactly the style you need.

Store Seasonal Clothes Elsewhere

There are professional organizers who would encourage you to keep all your clothes together in the same closet. They argue that seeing everything you have provides the mental reminder that you have enough and lessens the temptation to shop. I disagree with that idea because if you're practicing modern minimalism, you're already avoiding unnecessary shopping and have created storage solutions that prevent forgetting what you have. A clothes closet with open space around the in-season pieces positively impacts your mind. On the contrary, a full closet with every piece of clothing you own stuffed onto racks and into bins ignites stress.

Take your seasonal clothes and store them in labeled containers in a separate closet or on the highest shelves of your clothes closet. It's up to you to decide if you want clear or opaque containers. However, with proper labeling including a list of each item, you can create even cleaner lines in your closet with opaque containers.

In order to keep your seasonal items in the best shape, assess the threats from climate and bugs. If you live in a humid climate, invest in products that draw moisture out of the air. Keep these in the closet with the stored clothing items to prevent smells and mildew. Almost any climate is subject to moths and depending on where you store your seasonal items in your house, the threat may be higher. Cedar wood is excellent at repelling moths naturally. Cedar chests were popular for a reason. You can find cedar chips or finished balls at most home stores. They can be easily stored with your clothes in their containers.

Avoid the Diderot Effect

The Diderot Effect came from 18th century French philosopher Denis Diderot. He sought to explain the cause of overconsumption. He put forth the idea that if a consumer purchases one item, it can quickly spiral into more purchases and overconsumption. The Diderot Effect happens in every category of purchase, but it can easily ramp up when it comes to your closet. A gorgeous dress in a boutique window display calls you and before you know it, new shoes and a purse join it on the sales counter. You needed the shoes because nothing else you own matches and the purse was with the display begging to not be separated from the dress.

Find the byproducts of this phenomenon in your closet and get rid of them. In the future, keep in mind the pieces you already own and only add new pieces that fit in. Getting your closet to the point where you can easily see what you have will support this habit.

Keep One, Get Rid of the Rest

Everyone has duplicate clothing items in their closet. These pieces may vary slightly by color or style, but their function is the same. Look closely at what you have and decide how many you truly need. A sweater for every day of the week is too much for someone living in a climate that stays warm most of the year. You only need one pair of running shoes and to buy new ones when those wear out. Multiple winter jackets take up a lot of space and each require a cleaning at the end of the season. Find one in your closet that's a neutral color and wear it season after season.

The idea is to love everything you have in your closet. When you stock up on pieces with the same function, you inevitably end up with one you wear most often. Imagine making your closet into a space where you only have the items you wear all the time. Think about how much more satisfying it is to open the door and see only the items you love most. Keep that in mind as you go through and remove duplicate items from the space.

Physically Hold Each Item

It can be easy to rush through organizing your closet, especially as you get further into it and begin to question if there's a machine spitting out clothes behind your back. Don't let yourself rush this process. It's important to handle each item individually and assess its value in your closet. In doing so, you're allowing your mind the ability to process why you're keeping or getting rid of an item. Holding your favorite sweater from college will allow you to soak in the memories it triggers while also realizing the pilling is out of control and should be donated.

Give yourself that space to process the pieces in your closet. If it seems overwhelming to take on an entire closet at once, cut it into doses. Start with all your shoes, then all your dresses, then your jackets, and continue through the categories. Break it up to make the process easier and to allow you to look back on it with pride.

Keep Testing

If you still struggle to contain your clothes, try a different approach before diving into some of the steps above. Select about half the pieces in your wardrobe and put them away for one week (two if you can stand it!). During the week, dress yourself with what's left in your closet and note how many times you remember a particular piece that was stored away. You'll find that at the end of the period, most of the clothing hidden away did not cross your mind and its function was fulfilled by another piece.

If you found that to be the case, dive deeper into your wardrobe with some of the previous steps. The test shows how you can easily live with less and the steps laid out in this first section of the chapter show you just how to do it.

The intention of a minimalist closet is not to ration clothing like a scarce good, but to assemble the pieces you truly love. They are to be enjoyed and easily accessible in one place. In doing so, you're creating an aesthetically pleasing space that functions beautifully each day.

Garage or Storage Closet - Store With Intention

Everyone has a catch-all storage space in their home. If you're in a house, townhome, or condo that usually looks like a garage. For most apartments and condos, that looks like a storage closet sometimes within or just outside of the unit. Whatever it looks like for you, it is often the most overlooked space for practicing modern minimalism. However, if it is looked at as the one place minimalism doesn't apply it can fill up quickly with items from other rooms.

Start by finding your intentions for the space. Is it simply to store holiday decorations, out of season clothes, and your trusty tennis racket? Do you handle your own lawn maintenance and require a set of tools to get it done? Ask yourself what the space is to be used for and organize around that purpose (or set of purposes). A garage or storage closet should never be a place to keep things out of sight and thus out of mind. It has a purpose like every other room in your home.

Clear Out Your Space

Assess what you use your garage or storage space for and use that as your guide in clearing the clutter. If you are a home DIY guru, organize your supplies and get rid of old ones. If you haven't touched the golf clubs sitting in the corner since high school, donate them. Go through the stacked bins of holiday decorations and discard anything that is no longer functional. If you have duplicates of tools, pick the highest quality tool to keep. Get rid of the rest. Make sure to take into account other items from your home that will be stored in this space seasonally. Account for the space those items will need when organizing other items.

If you've been in your home for more than a year and there are unopened boxes in your garage or storage closet, they're most likely unnecessary. Go through the contents and get rid of the items no longer contributing to your life. Remember your purpose for the space and don't let clutter get in the way.

Vehicle Storage

One item that is often overlooked as a piece to get rid of is your vehicle. If you're living in a dense metropolitan area with more than a few transit options, this may be the right minimalist move for you. Freeing up the assigned parking space in your building's garage or opening your private garage can have positive effects on not only your home but your wallet, as well. You may save parking rent each month or find that with a garage cleared, you can convert the space into something more useful (like a guest room). The average car payment in the U.S. reached $554 a month in the first quarter of 2019.

When you weigh the costs and hassle of car ownership (insurance, parking fees, traffic tickets, maintenance) with adopting transit you might find car-free is the way to go. Consider the alternative modes of transportation which in major metropolitan areas now include scooters, bikeshares, buses, light-rail, trains, walkable neighborhoods, and even convenient cars for rent on most blocks. Start by replacing one trip a week with these alternatives and see how it fits into your lifestyle. A car-free lifestyle supports minimalism by giving you one less job to do throughout your day. Instead of avoiding fender benders on your way to work, you can enjoy a podcast or book on your bus commute. Getting out of the hassles associated with car ownership also supports calm and peacefulness in yet another aspect of your home life.

Store Everything Off The Floor

In garages and storage closets, piles of items are often the closest to organization you find. In both instances, valuable floor space is used up making it difficult to access everything when you need it. A garage that requires you to dig through and move things piled on the floor is not functional. Even more than that, it's stressful. Considering the work you have to put in just to get to the bins of holiday decorations can make you avoid the task at all costs.

Make organization easier in the space by committing to storing everything somewhere other than the floor. Invest in cabinetry or other storage that allows you to store, tools, bins, and other items together.

Consider the categories of items you've pared down to in the previous step and work out the logical storage layout. Power tools should definitely go together, but they should also be close to project materials that require them.

Find The Right Hierarchy of Storage

When you're putting together your storage system, take into consideration which items need to be the most accessible and which ones are used less often. Holiday decorations, seasonal clothes, specific tools, and other items should be stored up high. In doing so, you're creating easy access to the items you use more regularly. You're also creating a minimalist aesthetic that allows you to associate calm and peacefulness with the space. Be sure to label containers, even if they're behind cabinet doors. This will make it easy to identify what you have and where it is kept.

Carefully consider items that you've kept in the garage or storage closet to see if they should be stored elsewhere in your home. You might have seasonal items that should be stored in another closet or the attic where they would be closer to their final use. It's easy to overestimate the amount of space in a garage because they're so large and open. Approach it like you would any other room in your home. You will need to account for the space taken up by stored items, along with the space needed to conduct activities associated with the area.

The work you put into the other rooms in your home is supported when you take the time to declutter and organize your garage. By avoiding the usual pitfalls of using the garage space as a dumping ground for items you can't find a spot for elsewhere, you support your minimalist efforts in the rest of your home. By tackling both your closet and your garage in this chapter, the practice of modern minimalism in your home comes full circle. Remember to take these rooms one step at a time and give yourself the mental space to process every item you encounter.

Chapter 9. Minimalist Exterior
A Look You Never Thought Possible

Your front yard or balcony of your apartment is the first part of your home to greet you. Applying the principles of modern minimalism to this space supports the work you've done in the rest of your home. A minimalist yard is low-maintenance, potentially without a need to mow or water grass. It takes into account your climate and region with touches of the best native plants. Different textures come together to create an aesthetic that suits your unique terrain and home style. Practicing minimalism in your front yard brings together the calming feeling of open space with your unique style.

Your backyard is often a sanctuary in nature providing an escape from the indoors during warm weather months. It may also support you by growing food for consumption. It's visible from most rooms in the home and often that includes your bedroom. Its design should immediately disarm and put at ease anyone who steps out into it. There are features in both the front and backyard that will turn these spaces into a beautiful minimalist landscape. In the first part of this chapter, I'll share the features that distinguish a minimalist front yard and in the latter half provide tips to creating your dream minimalist backyard.

The Front Yard - A Calming Welcome Home

Curb appeal is an important aesthetic of any home. For your minimalist front yard, your goal should be to harness the current landscape to create curb appeal that is not only aesthetically pleasing, but evokes calm and peacefulness. As a gateway into the rest of your home, it's important to carefully assess your front yard and make the right changes. Below are the features that taken separately and together achieve the goal of a modern minimalist yard.

Feature 1: Native Plants

One of the outcomes of increased mobility over the last century and a half is the spread of plants to many different parts of the country and even the world. Plants that take off in areas where they are not native are considered an invasive species. Depending on the plant and its viability, it can distress the native plant life and create an imbalance in native wildlife dependent on those plants. A minimalist front yard will incorporate only native plants for the invasive species argument above as well as other important factors.

Native species thrive in their homes because of their ability to evolve and adapt to the conditions present. They're stronger as a result and can stand up to the climate in your region better than other plants. The market for native plants is strong making it easy to find experts in your area who not only sell native plants but offer knowledge and expertise. Take advantage of local independently owned greenhouses and landscape centers who can help you find the plants to fit your yard.

Be judicious with your selection of plants as it can be easy to overwhelm the softscape sections of your lawn. The softscape sections are the areas where plant life and softer elements reign. For each section, start small in your selection of plants to keep maintenance down and create space between each plant. A common feature of minimalist yards is the boxwood shrub. They're hearty and easily shaped to create clean lines as well as space between each one. Boxwoods have grown in popularity over time to the point where many different varieties have been bred to withstand a number of different climates. Refer back to the landscape experts at your local retailer to learn if there is a species of boxwood that's suited to your region and can live in harmony with native plants.

Feature 2: Limited Color Palette

This feature applies to both the plants and the architectural elements you bring into your yard. It's easy to clutter up your landscape design with the many variations of color available for purchase. Whether its plants or pavers, color can crowd your yard and take away the mental calm that comes from a streamlined design. One way to avoid falling into an endless bouquet of color is to plan out your yard in advance. Select the plants and types of textured features you are going to use beforehand.

There are professional landscape architects who specialize in planning the yard. If you choose not to hire a professional, you can still plan out what you need. Start from the perimeter of your home and work your way out. Consider the heights of your windows, the architecture of your porch, and the placement of your walkway as well as your driveway. Spend time measuring the size of the softscape areas so you can calculate the space needed between plants and thus how many fit in each area.

By taking this critical time to plan, you can identify not only how many of each feature you need, but the colors you'll be using. In this planning process, you can identify the colors you want and choose plants based on that palette. To keep the most minimal look, find only plants in the green color family. You can complement them with hard features such as stones, boulders, or pavers in a nude or tan color family.

Feature 3: Hardscapes

I've mentioned hard elements such as rocks or boulders a few times already. These elements provide a contrast to the softer ones and often stand on their own as a feature. In addition to things like rocks or pavers, hardscapes include elements such as walkways, driveways, patios, decks, and fencing. You may choose a yard that features hardscapes exclusively or integrate them with softscapes for a unique look. However you assemble your yard, take note of the variations in hardscape elements.

For a large yard, concrete provides a simple and effective look with easy maintenance. You can choose colored concrete in shades such as dark brown or a nude shade of tan. Concrete works best in driveways and walkways. For patios in large yards, consider paver bricks that can be assembled in clean line patterns. Crushed rock and gravel can also work in large yards to create a hardscape area that's aesthetically appealing and minimalist.

For a smaller yard, you'll have less maintenance and can get creative with crushed rock and gravel. You can use gravel in your driveway and then pavers in your walkway. A smaller yard can sustain concrete just as well as a larger yard, but don't be afraid to use other products to create hardscapes. Whatever you choose, make sure it balances well with the softscapes you use or the other hardscapes.

I mentioned fences and want to elaborate on their purpose in a front yard. They can create a more intentional feature when used against a blank wall of your home or serve a purpose as a perimeter feature. Horizontal slats in wooden fences create clean lines and pleasing visuals. You can also use metal in a neutral color, like black or brown, to add a different element to your yard.

Feature 4: Simple Furniture

Outdoor furniture has become elaborate in design over the last several years. Outdoor rugs the size of indoor area rugs have taken off as a must-have for your outdoor space. Furniture often requires cushions and is sold with throw pillows. The concept of bringing the indoors outside when it comes to comfort and features is admirable. However, it increases the maintenance if you have an area rug inside that needs to be cleaned as well as one outside. If you're stuck cleaning cushion covers and throw pillows of the dust from outside, the benefits they promise are cancelled out.

Furniture in your front yard should be sparse and intentionally selected for its function. Woods like teak and acacia provide the neutral colors needed to blend in with any style. Teak also stands up better to the elements providing style and functionality for years to come. Avoid a lot of clashing colors of the furniture and any accessories you may have. Choose simple, but comfortable, cushions if you require them. Consider how the furniture will complement the style of the yard and also provide functionality. If you have a wraparound porch, consider a separate seating area and adorning the other sections of the porch with simple neutral colored pottery. Be sure to leave space between each element (furniture and décor) to keep with the minimalist look.

Feature 5: Little to No Ornaments

Rather than clutter your yard with craft fair finds and mismatched birdbaths, choose only the best ornaments for your yard and get rid of the rest. Assess the best place in your yard for the pieces you keep and consider functionality in your decision to keep an item. A proper birdbath will invite more nature into the space while providing a complementary ornament that's pleasing to the eye. A neutral color container, like a vintage barrel, can provide visual appeal while also storing rainwater to be used for irrigation.

Making do with less ornamentation is not about clearing the yard of visual interest, but instead drawing the eye to the yard as a whole. Using neutral colors, clean lines, and sparse ornaments your attention is focused on the whole picture. If you have too many grabbing colors represented by too many objects, your mind jumps from one to another. Your yard should have an aesthetically pleasing and calming effect, not the opposite.

Feature 6: Grass-Free Zones

A minimalist yard should include minimal maintenance. The practice embraces native plants and simple furniture to support the low-maintenance label. Your front yard design can support this with either a grass-free yard or zones where hardscapes replace grass. You will need to consider city, county, or Homeowners Association rules about grass ratios. Once you have the requirements, take full advantage of those guidelines to minimize time spent maintaining your yard.

Grass that is not native to an area requires mowing, fertilization, weed control, and irrigation. Mowing may not take very long and is less frequent in dryer months, but the rest of the work to keep it green is enormous. Take back as much time as you can by cutting down on the square footage of grass. Alternatives to grass include hardscape features like rocks, planting native vines or other ground coverings, and even seeding native wildflowers. Wildflowers in particular are hardy and can grow within their native climate without much care. If you must have grass, whether through regulation or your desired aesthetic, find native grasses that thrive in your region. That will cut down on some of the maintenance associated with the typical specialty non-native grasses found in most yards.

Feature 7: A Water Feature

Your yard is the best representation of the earth element, so why not add in the water element as well? The sound of water is calming and would be a welcome sensory stimulation upon returning home after your day. For a front yard, consider open wall space to create a cascading feature that is the focal point. A simple fountain with clean lines can also stand alone in the midst of a hardscape foundation. A section of rocks with a concrete pad in the middle supporting a fountain is striking and achieves the desired effect. A backyard is also worthy of a water feature, but more on that in the next section.

Consider your front yard the first room in your home. It is the foyer through which you enter into the rest of your space. Treat it as such by taking your practice of minimalism to it and giving it the attention it deserves. Incorporating the above features based on the topographical, regional, and regulatory characteristics will give you the minimalist yard to match the rest of your home. Each feature can be adapted to the size and specifications of your yard. Even balconies and patios of apartments or condos can utilize some of the features above. As with every other room in your home, you need to assess your needs and what is feasible for you. Don't neglect this area of your home, build time to give it proper attention, starting with the simple act of decluttering.

The Backyard - A Garden To Remember

With the front yard sharing your style with the rest of the world, your backyard is a sanctuary in which you can retreat from the outside world. It should flow seamlessly from the sanctuary that is the inside of your home. It's a place to grow food for you and your family. A place to enjoy good weather. It helps balance your time spent indoors by inviting you to retreat into nature. Consider you and your family's needs as far an outdoor space and then plan from there. Like your front yard, your backyard should support your needs while also demanding the least amount of effort in the form of maintenance and upkeep. Landscape designer Julie Farris, based in New York, said it best: "Looking at your garden should not make you think of your to-do list." That statement is powerful and the goal to keep in mind as you plan your backyard.

Feature 1: Each Space Is Defined

In small and large yards alike, defining space positively impacts not only the aesthetic but the feeling of the yard. Define each space using materials that either match or contrast with the surrounding landscape. You may use pavers to define the space around a pool or other water feature. A wooden fence section can be used to support climbing plants and provide privacy. Bricks can be used to create raised beds delineating the plants from the hard or softscape feature that surrounds it. The concept of a raised bed has the space separation built in, you just need to choose the materials.

When defining the yard as a whole, consider the different materials that can be used to create privacy. Perhaps you want a green privacy feature using hardy native plants that grow quickly or can be purchased already mature. Wooden fences can be built and stained to match the color palette chosen for the backyard.

Feature 2: Privacy Abounds

I briefly touched on privacy when offering options for separating space, but the feature warrants its own section. Backyards are by their very name associated with privacy. Your home and land is situated to put the front yard as the face of the property leaving the backyard a bit of a mystery. Sometimes privacy is provided naturally by a nature preserve backing up to the property. It can also be provided by the geography of the rural region you reside. Oftentimes, you need to add your own privacy. It's an important feature to have no matter how it's created because a backyard's purpose is to provide a retreat.

Depending on your yard and the proximity of neighbors, you may only be able to provide privacy to one section of your yard. In order to do so, select the space that would provide the most benefit if privatized. It may be the patio just off the back door or a sanctuary between a few established trees beyond the house. After finding the space, consider the materials needed to create seclusion. If it is a screen porch connected to the house, consider utilizing a horizontal wooden fence for plants to climb. You can also install planters in an appealing pattern. Each fence section can stand independently allowing breezes to enter the porch while keeping visibility into the space to a minimum.

For a space in the yard not connected to the house, consider evergreens that can grow up around a thoughtfully arranged seating area. Using greenery versus another material helps camouflage your sanctuary space and keep it private. Evergreens would also work wonderful for spaces connected to the house if you're trying to keep the green color for continuity.

Feature 3: Hardscape Foundations

Hardscapes are just as important in the backyard as they are in the front yard. They often have even more impact because they take your focus off maintaining greenery and allow use of your backyard to the fullest extent.

If you're facing a large yard with a lot of greenery to maintain, consider starting at the exit to the house and let a hardscape feature ripple out covering more ground. If you have a deck off your house, start with laying a medium-sized rock or gravel around the perimeter. In the next ring, use small stone, and in the outer ring, use poured concrete. By laying the hardscape materials and extending the footprint of the deck, you are dedicating more space to a maintenance-free yard. This method can also be used for concrete patios or paver patios that extend off your home. I highlight this hardscape design specifically because it supports the goal for a backyard to flow seamlessly from the home.

Feature 4: Simple Designs

A helpful thought exercise is to look at your garden through the lens of Japanese garden philosophy. Imagine your yard as nature in miniature. Rather than an entire forest, you're planting a few trees. Instead of fields of wild grass, you've created sections where it can thrive in harmony with surrounding hardscape features.

The easiest way to keep it simple is define your neutral color palette before you start selecting features. Then, consider the needs of you and your family to define the purposes your yard will need to fulfill. The larger the yard, the more uses you can harness without stacking features on top of each other. "Simple" can seem like a loose term when you begin to consider the needs of a large family. There's no reason why a yard that needs to support kids' sports, dogs' activities, or entertaining regular guests can't be simple. It's all about how you approach it and the space you're given to work with. Rank the needs of your family and plan carefully how to fit them into the yard.

Feature 5: Raised Beds and Planters

Well-designed and made raised beds provide not only visual interest to your backyard but true functionality. Raised beds using bricks or pavers built wide allow for a place to sit while tending the garden. This design also keeps you from bending over for long periods of time while pruning or harvesting.

For the least amount of maintenance, use native plants carefully spaced to provide an appealing visual pattern. If you'd like your garden to support you and your family's food needs, a raised bed can provide easy access to harvests. Space seeds or seedlings carefully and don't overcrowd the bed.

Planters, or containers, can add visual appeal to your yard without requiring the work of clearing and tilling large parts of your yard for planting. You can control the soil without relying on what's naturally occurring in your yard thereby supporting strong healthy plants. Make sure you select containers that fit into a neutral color palette. You can also take advantage of seasons to change up greenery and color throughout the year.

Feature 6: Water Element

Backyards provide the perfect backdrop for large simple water features or small elaborate ones for you to enjoy. A pool is the perfect choice and may already be a part of the landscape depending on your region. In a pool area, it's important to keep pool accessories and toys out of sight. Keep a teak storage container nearby to quickly access anything you need for the pool. Opt for a monochromatic pool foundation color and use pavers or concrete to create a minimalist deck.

Fountains, whether part of a pool set up or standalone, contribute to the feeling of serenity your backyard should evoke. Be sure to keep the mechanical aspects out of sight and consider fountain options that put reservoirs into the ground. By having the fountain reservoirs just below the surface, the transition from yard to fountain is seamless. You can find the materials yourself for a fountain build or consult an expert for an easy to install feature.

Your backyard is part of the natural flow of your home. It should seamlessly blend with your home providing privacy, usefulness, and a sense of calm. Upon entering your backyard, you should feel at ease and see the features as complementary of one another. Each feature in this section contributes to the perfect minimalist backyard. Take time to assess your family's needs, yard size, and materials at hand to create a retreat from daily life right in your home.

There's a reason modern minimalism is often referred to as a practice. It is an ongoing experiment in finding ways to best enhance your life. Rather than achieving an enhanced life by consuming and cluttering your home, modern minimalism uses a specific set of tools to create space in your home that in turn creates space in your mind. Its purpose is not to trade in all your materials for a desolate space, but to sharpen your focus on the things and experiences that matter most. In your practice, you find mental clarity and space that can be reallocated to finding your own highest and best purpose.

Conclusion

You picked up this book because you've attempted minimalism before, have heard about it, or because a large change in your life has brought you to the practice. I count myself as a member of the latter. However you found your way to this book, it's for you. It's not here to promise a quick fix or a solution to everything that's going on in your life. It's here to help you bring minimalism into your home and free up the space in your mind taken up by clutter. By aligning yourself with the objects in your life, you're able to more easily tackle other areas of life.

I put this book together because of how much minimalism has helped me. I've seen firsthand the positive effects of ridding my home of clutter. There's the immediate rush of walking into a clean room the first few times. What surprised me, however, is the lasting impact on my mood from practicing minimalism. In each space, I've organized the items and set up tools that make it easy to keep what I initially set up. Tasks like laundry, dishes, or cleaning no longer feel like "must do" chores but simply routines that provide real benefit. Everything in this book has helped me focus on my own purpose and even deal with the difficult valleys of life. I know it can do the same for you.

Taking each chapter separately, it might seem difficult to envision their ability to align your mind with the objects in your home. Wrapped up together, it becomes clear the ways in which space between clothes hanging in the closet and planters in the backyard combine to give you a neutral space to just *be*.

Dedicating time to each room in your home and setting it up to best support you is the best kind of self-care. You're sacrificing a little time now to open up your future to every possibility. You're ensuring that peace, calm, and serenity remain a part of your lifestyle for years to come.

Each chapter is ordered to maximize your entry or re-entry into the practice of modern minimalism. Each meant to be referenced again and again throughout your practice. While some solutions are meant for specific spaces, there are a few common tools and mindsets to keep with you at all times:

- Clutter is enemy number one to your sanity and your practice. It takes up space in your mind as well as your home.

- Use mechanisms given to stem the flow of clutter and prevent it from piling up. These include rethinking how you shop and what you buy. Your organization in each room will also keep clutter down.

- Be honest about your needs and desires in each room. Not everything in your home is useful or positively contributing to a peaceful mind. Honesty up front means you're less likely to repeat decluttering and organizing in the near future.

- Each space has its purpose and each purpose has its space. Our homes support a variety of needs depending on our lifestyle. Give each important part of your life the space it needs to support you.

- Make space between objects in every room. This simple action has immediate effect, even if you're just beginning your practice.

- If you haven't used something recently, you're not likely to use it again in the near future. Send it on its way knowing that you can get another one if you need it. Maybe someone else could use it.

- If a room or situation overwhelms you, start small. Minimalism is a marathon, not a sprint. You need to get to the end at your own pace.

I want you to end this book feeling like there are options and tools that fit your lifestyle. We do not all live in the same type of dwelling. Size and location as well as renting versus owning will affect how you practice minimalism. The practice is not just for people who can afford an Eichler-designed home in the Bay Area of California. It's for a young grad student living in the middle of a university town. It's for the recent grad who traded more space for a central location in a walkable neighborhood. It's for retirees and families who want to get a handle on the clutter life accumulated. No matter your situation, each chapter has you in mind. Refer back often to the chapters and sections that speak to you and your dwelling.

This book is meant to be picked up again and again. It will travel with you through life and through the stages of your practice. These pages contain the solutions to break down every barrier preventing you from living your life to its fullest purpose. Take with you the powerful knowledge that you are capable and deserving of each and every benefit found in a modern minimalist lifestyle. You're worth the work to find peacefulness, calm, and serenity in every room of your home. You're worthy and capable, no matter what anyone says. You've reached the end of this book, but you're at the beginning of a new chapter in your life. Live it well.